DRAWERS FOR YOUR MONEY

Nir Sadeghan
Drawers For Your Money

Published by Spines Publishing Platform
ISBN: 979-8-90222-050-3

Spines

DRAWERS FOR YOUR MONEY

PRACTICAL BANKING GUIDE TO INCREASE FINANCIAL WELLNESS

NIR SADEGHAN

CONTENTS

DEDICATION

I would like to take the time to dedicate this book to my family, coworkers, and clients. I want to say that without the valuable knowledge and experience that I gained from everyone involved in my life, I wouldn't be able to write this book. I also want to dedicate this book to God and thank Him for the ability He gave me to write this book. Thank you all for assisting me in this journey and giving me the strength and ambition to write this book. Those who know, it took me many years to write this book, and there were many hurdles and tribulations in my life that prevented me from getting it done. However, dedication and support from those closest to me have helped me overcome the times that I considered giving up on this book. At times, the project was shelved for months and sometimes years at a time. However, I always knew that I must finish this book because the information that is contained in it is important for people to

make better choices regarding their financial wellness. It is important because people need to understand how banks work, how mortgages work,
how credit works, and the ins and outs of financing a loan. These and many other topics are covered in this book, and it must be shared. Therefore, I am dedicating this book to the people who stuck with me on this journey; even though you are very few, you know who you are. Thank you for believing in me and giving me the strength to finish this book!

ACKNOWLEDGMENTS

First and foremost, I want to acknowledge God and his greatness for creating me and giving me the ability to write this book so that I could do my part to help humanity in a very minute and small manner. The whole purpose of this book is for people to acquire knowledge so that they can better their lives financially. I wrote this book with a desire to contribute to financial literacy rather than as a tool for personal financial gain.

I want to acknowledge all of the people that I have worked with throughout the years who gave me the knowledge base and wisdom to write this book. Your mentorship and guidance are a testament to your own knowledge and awesomeness!! I am sure that I have much more to learn from my colleagues in the coming years. My thirst for knowledge is ever-growing, and learning from you all is both an honor and a privilege.

I would like to acknowledge you, the reader, for purchasing this book and valuing the knowledge in it. I hope that you will gain something by reading this book and appreciate the effort and time invested in putting it together.

Lastly, I would like to thank my clients! I want to thank you for asking me the tough questions; for not cutting me slack, for believing in me, and last but not least, for trusting me enough to become my customer or client. The majority of my knowledge came from my customers and their needs and wants. Their requirements always made me pursue the perfection that I always seek, and I am sure that going forth, I will learn much more from my clients and make additions and revisions to this book as new knowledge becomes available. As we all know, the only constant is change, and as time goes by, many things will change in the banking, finance, and financial markets; and when that change arrives, I will do whatever it takes to keep abreast and make the changes in this book with updated editions and revisions.

INTRODUCTION

My name is Nir Sadeghan. I was born in Tehran, Iran, in 1977. In 1979, when I was two years old, my parents left Iran due to the Islamic Revolution. My parents decided to move to the USA, and we settled in Detroit, Michigan. When I was about six years old, my family moved again, this time to Israel. We resided in Israel until I was fourteen years old. My family moved to the USA again, this time the destination was Los Angeles, CA. Just by reading the first part of my introduction, you can see that I didn't have a stable life. My life was all about moving from one place to another, and as a result, my background is both diverse and eclectic.

I am the eldest of three brothers, and once we moved to the USA, I started high school in a Jewish private school and completed my high school studies in a public institution. After high school, I took a break for a couple of months and decided to travel back to Israel. It was a major crossroad for me when I went to Israel because I was contemplating whether to stay and join the Israeli military or come back to the United States to attend college. I chose the latter, and that's when my adventure with the banking world began.

I started in banking in 1999, and before that, I worked for a restaurant as a delivery boy and dishwasher. My next job was at Michael's Arts and Crafts as a cashier and later a cashier supervisor. I started my banking career after I accompanied my girlfriend at the time to a Home Savings of America bank branch, where she had certain banking business to conduct. The banker who spoke to me asked if I'd be interested in possibly working for a bank, and I said sure. After that, everything else is history.

I started as a teller and worked my way up to different roles at the bank. My most accomplished role was in helping build a wholesale mortgage division at an online bank I used to work for. The knowledge I gained and am still gaining as a result of banking is evident in this book, and it is from real-life experiences. I am still active in the financial industry, and I also work in Medical Sales. I have always believed that the people who work in their respective fields are the ones who have the best knowledge, and it is crucial that the knowledge they have is shared for others to learn from and implement in their lives. I also hold it true that the people who share knowledge in their respective fields and those who share their knowledge in any form are the best people to learn from; the reason is that there are many authors out there that theorize things and make claims that don't have practical application in real life.

After noticing a lack in practical banking guidance that wasn't overly complicated for the average banker, I decided it was time to share my knowledge.

I decided to write this book for two reasons: not only did I want to pull from my mental arsenal to help others make better financial decisions, while helping them gain a better understanding of the banking world and how banking and personal finance are interconnected. In a world that is ever-changing; banking is also at the forefront of change, and many of our dreams and aspirations are connected to banking. Whether we have a dream of purchasing a house, going on a vacation, or saving for our children's college funds; banking is involved in our lives in one way or another. Therefore, I took on the task of explaining to the masses how banks work and how they could use banks to their advantage. If I were able to pass even a small piece of information on to each individual who reads this book, and they were able to implement these strategies into their daily lives, then this book is a success in my opinion. The second reason I wrote this book is because in 2008, there was a huge mortgage meltdown, and the US government started bailing out many banks, which angered many people. Many people lost their life savings, their homes, and their livelihoods. I was one of those victims as well. I was laid off from a job that I truly loved and was passionate about in the mortgage wholesale industry. When the mortgage meltdown happened, I lost my job and was forced to file for bankruptcy in 2009. Like many people who filed for bankruptcy at that time, I did it to save my house. However, the events of 2008 fueled a passion in me to write this to educate people about the banking system and how they could use banks to their advantage.

This book is a practical guide for people to use in their lives when it comes to banking and personal finance. My goal in writing this book is to help people manage their finances and money in a way that is applicable to their daily lives. This book's goal is to help people avoid land mines in banking and give them the knowledge they need when they want to take out a loan or open an account. This book will give you the tools to better manage your accounts and give you a better understanding of how banks function and what their role is in our society.

This book is not your typical financial literacy book, where other authors give you an overview of how things work and where you can find information, leaving you to your own devices. This book actually gives you real-life instructions on how you can use your bank accounts to correspond to your personal financial budget, and it will give you information and knowledge to deal with banks when you want to take out a loan or open a bank account.

This book will be a gateway for people to look at their finances in a new light and help them manage their money and credit in a more productive way. I have included real financial planning tools, unlike the traditional financial planning that people are accustomed to, where they meet with someone and end up getting a life insurance policy or annuity. With this book, you can actually do real financial planning and incorporate life insurance and annuities as well. I hope that you will enjoy this book, and if I was able to teach you one practical idea that you were able to use in your life, then I did my job, and this book has served its purpose!

HOW BANKS WORK

To understand how banks work, it's important that we know some of their history and how banks became an integral part of our lives. I am not about to give you a history lesson, but rather a quick synopsis of how banks started. We can date banking to ancient times as far as the Babylonian times in the second millennium B.C. We can find evidence of banking in the Code of Hammurabi, which is the earliest known code of law. Money as we know it today was not present in those times. People used cattle, grain, or other crops, and eventually precious metals, to make deposits. A wide range of deposits was made, and loans were made with interest, just like today. We could also find similar banking activities in ancient Egypt. However, in ancient Egypt, they used to store grains in centralized storage houses, and people would use written orders as a means of payment for a certain amount of grain. The system that was established by the Egyptians worked so well that even after coinage and precious metals were introduced into banking, they still used this system.

Modern-day banking started in medieval Italy in the cities of Florence, Venice, and Genoa. The main activities they engaged in were financing the lavish lifestyles of the royal family and financing the wars they would engage in. Furthermore, they provided loans to merchants engaged in international trade. The two most dominant families in Florence in the 14th century were the Bardi and Peruzzi families. These two families met their demise when they tried financing King Edward's 100-year war against France, which resulted in King Edward defaulting on all the loans he took from those two families.

One of the most recognized and influential figures in banking was Giovanni Medici. He was the founder of the Medici bank in 1397. The Medici family has had many years of experience as money changers, and it was this family that moved from an ordinary table in the market-place to a building where they started conducting banking activities, thus creating the brick-and-mortar building concept that banks conduct business from to this day. The Medici banking empire expanded throughout Europe with branches reaching as far as London. With the most distinguished customer of the Medici bank being the Pope.

Many of the business transactions conducted by banks

internationally required banks to use bills of exchange. This simple method provided merchants a bill for repayment at a later date. The church at that time had a prohibition on charging interest, so banking played a major role in trade. Banks would provide a bill of exchange in one currency and would collect payment in a different currency, essentially avoiding the church's prohibition of collecting interest.

A major development happened in the 17th and 18th centuries when the British and Dutch improved on their banking practices. It started with local goldsmiths who were the forefathers of frictional banking; we will be explaining this method in great detail later in the chapter. After the Civil War demand for goldsmiths was nonexistent. In order to survive, these goldsmiths decided to resort to storing precious metals in safes as a means of generating income. What they started to do was store precious metals for people and then issue a receipt to the people who stored those precious metals with them in their vault. At first, these receipts acted as currency. However, as time passed, the goldsmiths realized that since not all the people who deposited those precious metals with them would ask for them back all at once, the goldsmiths started to issue additional receipts, which later became currency.

As far as the history of banks in the United States goes, the first bank was established in 1781 in the state of Philadelphia. By 1794, the United States had 17 more banks in its territories. Banking in the United States was strictly issued by the federal government; however, the state of New York, in the year 1838, adopted the free banking act, which allowed any individual to conduct banking business as long as they met the state's legal criteria. After the Civil War, the Federal government stepped in and passed legislation that provided banks with a federal charter. This allowed banks to issue notes with backing from the government. This legislation also brought all banks under federal supervision.

This was a quick summary of the history of banking and how banking was born. I will now explain the role that banks play in modern-day and how they impact the economy here in the United States.

When someone thinks of banking, the first thing that comes to mind is brick-and-mortar buildings with tellers and bankers taking deposits and opening accounts. However, the truth is that banks play a pivotal role in our daily lives. Banks have a major influence over government and policy making, which, after reading this chapter, will clarify many things that are not taught in schools. Furthermore, banks store our money, lend our money, invest our money, and manufacture money.

To better explain this, I am going to break banking into two segments: the macro and the micro aspects of banking. I will be explaining these two aspects in great detail and this will clarify how banks control many of our daily activities. First, we need to understand the macro part of banking and how banks work in the grand scheme of things. To begin to explain the macro part of banking, we must understand that banks manufacture money, and that is their main source of income.

Many of us know that banks take our deposits and lend them back to the general public at a higher interest rate than they pay on our deposits. That is good and dandy, but that is not how they really conduct business. Banks engage in the practice of fractional banking, which in turn makes them manufacturers of money and creators of money from thin air. The process is as follows: Because banks act as money factories, they need money as raw material. So, the question now becomes, where do they get this money to produce more money? The answer is from the general public deposits that are made into the bank on a daily basis. It is really important to understand one important thing here, and that is that banks don't only gain profits from the services they provide, but they create money that never existed before. To illustrate this, we are going to use the following example. Mr. Joe Smith goes to the bank and deposits $100,000 into a certificate of deposit at 5%. The bank now has the ability to lend Mr. Smith's money to someone else. This is where the government steps in. The Federal Reserve sets a reserve rate of 3%- 10%. So, if the bank has a 3% reserve rate, the bank must keep 3% of Mr. Smith's $100,000 on reserve, which is $3,000. So the bank is left with $97,000 to lend to the public. If the reserve rate for the bank which is set by the

Federal Reserve, is 10%, then the bank would have to keep $10,000 on reserve and lend the remaining $90,000. To keep things simple, let's assume that the reserve rate for our bank is 10%. So the bank now loaned $90,000 of Mr. Smith's $100,000 deposit and kept $10,000 on reserve. We'll call this loan #1. This transaction is the most critical point for the bank as the role of manufacturing money. What has happened here is that on the balance sheet of the bank this $90,000 is considered an asset for the bank and not a liability as many would think (the liability is for the borrower since the borrower has to pay the loan back to the bank), Because the bank has a lien on the property, this loan is considered an asset for the bank and that is what the bank reports on their balance sheet, $90,000 in assets.

So, what has happened here, in essence, is that the bank has created or manufactured money. The process doesn't stop here because the bank has created an asset; the bank now has the power to lend additional money based on this new asset that was created! Since the same Federal Reserve rules apply to this new asset, the bank must keep 10% on reserve, which means that the bank can only lend 90% of the $90,000 or $81,000. That would be considered loan number two. By creating another loan, the bank has in essence created another asset for itself and, in turn, has created new money that never existed before. This now gives banks the ability to lend additional money. All they have to do is keep 10% of the $81,000 on reserve, which would leave them with $72,900 that the bank could be lending out. This loan would be loan # 3. Federal Reserve rules allow the bank to repeat this process up to five or six times based on the original $100,000 deposit that we used in our example. Each loan that the bank makes creates an asset for the bank, which in turn becomes lendable money, and new money is manufactured.

After this explanation, you might be in shock, but this is the truth. Banks have been doing this for many years with full government banking. We have all heard the term run on the bank. That is the worst nightmare any bank or country could face. The reason is that if every single individual decides to withdraw their money from the banks, the banks won't have enough money to give out, since they are "banking" on the fact that there won't be a run on the bank. That is a reason the federal government came up with the FDIC, which is an acronym for the Federal Deposit Insurance Corporation. The federal government created this institution to give the general public some peace of mind regarding our money to avoid runs on the bank in times of distress. One major reason why banks fail in this country is when banks don't know how to manage their balance sheets correctly and manage their reserve requirements correctly. I could be writing about this subject for a whole book, and people have written books extensively about fractional lending and how banks control our daily lives.

However, this book is just a practical guide to banking providing general knowledge. A simple Google search would give you a treasure trove of information about fractional banking and how banks work on the macro level.

I will now explain the micro part of banking, and that is the most relevant information that touches every single individuals daily life, whether they bank for their personal needs, business needs, or any other banking need. We have all stepped into a bank to conduct some sort of business or another. This section will discuss the basic operations of a branch and what to look for when you walk into a branch, and how a branch operates. I will be using examples from major banks that I have worked for and visited. It is very possible that different banks in different states have different ways of conducting business; however, they all have the same underlining purpose, and that is gaining your business and your deposits.

When an individual walks into a branch, you will most likely see the teller section and the banker section. In the banking world, the teller section is called operations, and the banker section is where new accounts are opened and customers account issues are addressed. The teller section mainly deals with customer deposits, withdrawals, and transfers between accounts, converting currency, and many other operational technicalities.

The tellers are the most high-touch employees of the bank. They are the first people we see when we walk into the bank. Their responsibilities include executing your transaction and answering questions regarding your account within their scope of knowledge. The tellers are mainly order takers. Good relationships with tellers are crucial. After the tellers, you have the lead tellers or supervisors. The difference between them and the tellers is that they often have higher limits and can make overrides on whether to place checks on hold or not. They also help in determining the lunch schedules of the tellers and help with the balancing of tellers' cash drawers and other operational activities. Next, you have the operation managers who are in charge of making sure the vault is balanced and that there are enough tellers at any given moment during bank operating hours.

Then you have the banker who usually opens accounts, takes straight deposits, answers customer inquiries about account issues, and develops relationships. Cultivating a good relationship with a banker is crucial, and I will discuss this in the next chapter. Then you have the premier bankers who are licensed bankers; in most cases, they usually deal with people who have larger balance accounts. They also deal with securities products. The business banker is in charge of opening business accounts and addressing business owners' account issues. Business bankers have the ability to refer larger businesses to commercial bankers to better assist them. The private banker usually deals with clients who have high net worth and are accredited investors. An accredited investor is someone who has a net worth of one million dollars or a joint net worth of one million dollars with their spouse. They can also be making two hundred thousand dollars a year for the past two years and are on schedule to make the same amount in the current year, or three hundred thousand dollars with their spouse for the past two years and are on schedule to make the same amount in the current year. We also have the assistant branch manager who oversees and makes sure all the bankers are meeting their daily sales goals and handles any customer issues or complaints. You then have the branch manager who oversees all branch activities and handles customer issues and concerns as well. The branch manager conducts daily, weekly or monthly branch meetings to make sure the branch is operating to everyone's satisfaction, this includes assessing customer service and satisfaction.

Knowing your way around the bank is extremely important. When I used to work at the bank, I would come across many people who would come into the bank and didn't know where to start or who to see. I will be making this easy for you by breaking down the issues, and you will most likely have to see a different individual for different needs. I will only address the major issues people usually ask for when they walk into a branch. When people want to open an account, they should always seek a banker or a premier banker. Premiere bankers are in many cases licensed with their Series 6 and 63 licenses and can offer advice on securities products such as mutual funds, retirement accounts, health savings accounts, and anything that has to do with securities. If you would like to open a business account, you should always seek a business banker. If you have large sums of money, then you should always seek a private banker. All private bankers have a securities license and can give you advice on securities-based products and services that can produce larger rates of returns with higher risk. I will go into much detail regarding this in chapter ten.

Many people would come to the bank with issues they had with fees on their accounts. Since the new banking regulations that were passed in 2009, banks have little to no room to reverse fees. However, there are a few ways of getting your fees reversed, and that is by calling the bank's 800 number and asking them to reverse the fee. If that doesn't work, then you can also try speaking to the branch manager. I will discuss in the next chapter how a good relationship with your banker can help with this matter. In chapter four, you will learn how to avoid overdraft fees altogether.

If you have questions regarding trust accounts, IOLTA accounts, and more complicated accounts, you should always seek a premier banker, and if need be, the premier banker can always refer you to other individuals within the bank if it is necessary.

People always come to the bank asking for statements, the last five transactions, and balances of their accounts from the tellers; when people do that, they hold up the line and make people wait in line longer. With a few clicks on your mouse, you can get your account statement online and avoid the trip to the bank. Also, instead of waiting in line for statements, transaction history, or balances, or any other issue, always ask the banker if they can help, and they will. This way you might learn something new about your account or a new product the bank has to offer that might benefit you. This way, you will also have the opportunity to review your account and see if you fit in a better account that would accommodate your needs.

On many occasions, business owners or individuals would ask the bankers about tax issues or legal issues. These questions are not appropriate for the bankers to answer. The answer to tax issues or legal issues regarding your account should always be asked of your accountant or lawyer.

The one issue that is really important to address is when people experience fraud on their accounts. When people have had their account information compromised, it is always advisable for them to go to the bank and speak to a banker immediately and explain the nature of the fraud. Banks always protect your account one hundred percent against fraud or theft, so you don't have to worry about losing money. The process of resolving all issues might be frustrating in the beginning, but with patience and a good banker, everything works out. In some cases you don't have to close your account, and a simple claim will suffice. In other cases, you might have to open a new account, it all depends on the nature of the case. One thing I always advise is not to immediately close your account if you have direct debits or direct credits. I always advise people to open a new account and transition to the new account before closing their existing account. This will save you many headaches and problems if you were to close your account that same day.

You will at times find that different banks operate in different manners. For instance, in smaller community banks the bankers take your deposits and make cash transactions as well as open new accounts. Some banks operate online only. A description of the types of banks will be given in a later chapter. What I wrote in this chapter is a description of traditional banking by major banks.

To sum everything up in this chapter, you have learned how banks started, their grand scheme of the role they play in our economy, their importance in our economy, and lastly, the structure by which banks operate on the branch level. To learn more about the bank's macro effect on our economy, I highly recommend people research the way banks affect our daily lives online. Banks have a major influence on government, media, and cultural issues in today's society. Saying this, I implore people to research the role banks have in our lives on a daily basis.

Now that you've learned more about the history of

banks, I want you to take time to measure your financial literacy.

How much do you already know about money acquisition? Money management and banking?

Take this short quiz below. These are six basic financial literacy principles that you should know.

Financial Literacy Quiz (Published on Forbes.com)

1. As a general rule, how many months' expenses do financial planners recommend that you set aside in an emergency fund?

a. 1 to 3 months
b. 3 to 6 months
c. 6 to 12 months
d. 12 to 15 months

Correct Answer: The correct answer is C, which is "6 to 12 months.

2. If you have too many credit cards, what should you do?

a. close as many as possible
b. request a higher credit limit
c. be cautious about closing credit cards · d) close the cards with the lowest balances

Correct Answer: The correct answer is C, which is "be cautious about closing credit cards."

3. If a late payment is sent to a collections agency, how long will it remain on your credit history even if you have paid it off?

a. less than a year
b. 1 to 3 years
c. 4 to 5 years
d. 6 to 7 years

Correct Answer: The correct answer is D, which is "6 to 7 years."

4. What is the formula for calculating your net worth?

a. assets minus liabilities
b. liabilities minus assets
c. assets plus liabilities
d. assets divided by liabilities

Correct Answer: The correct answer is A, which is "assets minus liabilities."

5. Imagine that the interest rate on your savings account was 1% per year and inflation was 2% per year. After one year, would your ability to buy something with the money in this account be:

a. more than today
b. less than today

c. exactly the same
d. don't know

Correct Answer: The correct answer is B, which is "less than today."

6. Which of the following about Federal student loans is NOT true?

a. For certain federal loan programs, the interest on your loan is paid by the government while you are in school or during grace periods.
b. Your parents must sign a promissory note before loan funds are distributed.
c. Entrance loan counseling for all first-time borrowers is required.

Correct Answer: The correct answer is B, which is "your parents must sign a promissory note before loan funds are distributed."

YOUR RELATIONSHIP WITH YOUR BANKER AND TELLER

This chapter is a key chapter. It discusses the importance of developing a relationship with your teller and your banker, and why it is important, and how it will help you resolve issues you might have in the bank. As you might know, I learned one important lesson in life, and that is that it is not what we know in life that will help us succeed necessarily, but who we know! The people we know and the relationships we develop in life are the ones that will make all the difference in our lives and determine each individual's level of success in life. That also holds true in banking. The people you know in the bank and the relationship you establish with them are crucial in obtaining your goals when you need help with issues that might arise. In this chapter, I will be giving tips on how to know if you have the right banker and how to choose the right banker for your needs. When banking, it is really important that you have the right key people "working for you." This will help you tremendously every time you need something from the bank.

The first thing you should do when you are shopping for a bank is interview a few bankers and ask them questions. Another way of getting to know a good banker is by getting referrals from your friends and family. Often, the business that bankers get is from referrals, so it is really important for the banker to establish a relationship with their customers so they can earn their customers' referrals.

I have mentioned that when you choose a banker, you should interview them and ask them a few questions. I am going to give you some questions to ask your banker, so you know that you are in good hands. The first question you should always ask is: How long have you been in banking? The time they have been in banking is crucial because their knowledge base is broader and their connections in the bank are stronger. The next question you should ask is about them as a person. Get to know your banker, find common ground and see if you have good chemistry with your banker. Test your banker's knowledge by asking him challenging questions about bank products and services. If the banker is unsure of a question and you see him go ask the manager, that is when you know the banker has a good relationship in the bank. With this in mind, ask your banker about their relationship with their manager and coworkers, and if you might need future help from those people, would he be able to direct you to those individuals quickly and effectively? There are several questions that you could be asking your banker; use common sense, and you will be successful in choosing the right banker that suits your needs and banking goals.

After you have opened your account, you will most likely be conducting business in the bank, like making deposits, withdrawing, and transferring funds. You will be doing all these transactions with the teller or lead teller. I highly recommend that you get to know the tellers on a first-name basis. If you do so, they will go far and beyond to help you when you need their help with issues that might arise for you in the future. Develop a relationship with your tellers so that if you ever have any issues with holds or new staff, they could help you get over those issues. The relationships you develop with the bank tellers are crucial because they are the ones who can help you resolve issues with your accounts in a time of need.

Also, as you get to do business in the bank, pay attention to the way the teller talks to their superiors and the relationship they have with them. This will help you in case you might have an issue with your transaction, because the teller could, in some cases, help tilt the situation to your favor. So get to know your teller's name and develop a relationship with them, because you never know one day that relationship might come in handy.

We would never think that having a good relationship

with our banker is crucial. However, the relationship we develop with our banker is very important, and that is because we are talking about our money. Money today is really important, and it is a way for us to get what we need to conduct our daily routines and activities. I believe that if we got to know our bankers like we got to know our doctors and lawyers, then our experiences in the bank would be much more pleasant. That is why I always recommend people to stick to one banker and deal with one person at the bank. Now you might ask what happens if my banker is not at the bank, and I have some business that can't wait? That is a very valid question. A good banker would always refer another banker as a point person for you, just in case they are not there. Loyalty to your banker is really important as well. When you show your banker loyalty by opening accounts only with your banker or going to your banker when you have issues, you are telling that banker that you value him/her and when you have an issue, that banker will go out of his/her way to help you accomplish what you need to get done. In certain cases, more often than not, bankers move to other branches, get promoted, get fired, quit, or move to a different bank. If the banker moved to another branch, and the distance is reasonably close. I recommend you stick to that banker in their new branch. If they got promoted and they can still help you, then stick to them; if not, ask them for someone that they trust will assist you in doing your business in the bank the same way they did.

If they got fired, then find a new banker based on the guidelines I mentioned above. If they quit or move to a different bank, I recommend that you find out which bank they work for now and visit them in their new bank, and if you have a good relationship with them, they will tell you if it would be worth it for you to switch over or open an additional account in their bank.

As we go through the circle of life, our needs change, and so do our banking needs. What we needed when we were in college won't hold true when we are retired. That is why it is very important that we ask our banker to refer us to the right individuals in the bank to help us with ever-changing situations in our lives that may affect our banking needs. Our banker won't be able to help us with every single product and service that the bank has to offer; therefore, the individuals and connections our banker has are really important. Make sure you choose a banker who has those connections and relationships, so when the time comes, you have the right team that will help you accomplish your business in the bank.

The relationships we cultivate with our bankers are extremely important because the banks are holding our money, and we trust them with that responsibility. Therefore, the people we come in contact with in the bank are the people we must trust with our money. The relationship you develop with the tellers, bankers, and other personnel is important for different reasons, but the most important reason is for you to accomplish what you came to do in the bank. Who knows, maybe the relationship you develop with the bank employee could develop into a friendship as well. Just remember one thing, the bank employee is a human just like anybody else, and they want to earn your business so you can continue to do business with the bank, so he/she can keep their job.

Let's discuss some facts about relationships and currency here. Let's examine the correlation between managing your emotions and your relationships.

Relationship currency can give you the ability to:

1. request something or some action of someone else;
2. get access to other relationships; and, as we discussed with regard to performance currency,
3. recover from a mistake. There are things that you may not know or have a solution for, but someone you have access to may have the answer or access to a solution.

CREDIT

While working in the bank, I would often get many people who would ask me about credit. I would get all sorts of questions like: What do you use credit for? How do you build credit? And most commonly, how do you acquire it?

To begin, I want to say that credit has to be used responsibly, and credit is not a means to pay bills, to buy groceries, or to purchase daily necessities. This is where most people get in trouble with credit, and they ruin their credit health. Many people believe that credit is a right that was given to them and that they must have it. However, many people forget that credit is extended by the private sector via banks, credit unions, private individuals, and corporations, in some cases. These institutions or individuals have guidelines that they follow and establish in order to minimize their risk of loss from people who might not pay their obligation, and in order to minimize their risk, they often use the FICO score, also known as the Fair Isaac Corporation. FICO scores are determined by several factors. Having the right balance of credit on your report is essential to a good FICO score. For example, if someone has too many credit lines (a credit line is any obligation that an individual has to pay another individual or institution), it could affect that person's FICO score in a negative manner. Furthermore, if someone hasn't paid their obligations on time, then that could also affect their credit score in a negative manner. Therefore, having the right balance of credit is crucial in maintaining a healthy FICO score.

The first question, as you recall, was what is credit for? Well, credit is a means to purchase items that will help us with our goals in life and ultimately our financial success. If used wisely, credit can be a powerful tool and a way to build wealth. Credit is a means for individuals to achieve greater goals, such as purchasing or leasing a car, buying real estate, or an RV, etc. I am going to state something that has not been tested scientifically, but I have seen and have come across many people who have used credit for everyday purchases and have gotten in trouble because they purchased beyond their means, and when the time came to pay that credit card bill, they didn't have enough to cover their credit expense. Therefore, it is extremely important to remember that credit is not a means to live off of, but a means to achieve greater goals in life. Now, I do understand that some credit card companies do offer rewards and cash back if you make purchases with their credit cards; however, it is very important to make sure you don't overspend. If you spend within your means on a credit card and manage your payments in a responsible manner, then it is a great way to take advantage of the perks credit card companies have to offer. However, if you don't have self-discipline, I don't recommend using credit cards for daily use.

The second and third questions I would get are: How do you build credit, or how do you start building credit? And where do you get it? Those are million-dollar questions, and if anything, the knowledge that I am going to share with you now is worth a million dollars and has paid for this book tenfold. As you know, credit is extended largely by financial institutions to individuals. I spoke briefly about credit and FICO scores; however, there has to be a starting point for individuals to start building their credit, and this is where many people get lost or confused. They just don't know where to start when they want to build their credit. I am going to show you the easiest ways someone could establish a credit file. The first way is to piggyback with someone who already has an established credit report. Well, you are probably asking what it means to piggyback. It's simple, let's assume that you are a young lad and you just turned eighteen, and you are working and going to school, now you want to buy a car. But you can't finance the car because you don't have credit, so you need to build credit. What you can do is ask one of your parents to add you to their credit cards and start building credit that way. That is a quick example of piggybacking on someone else's credit file. Now, another way of establishing credit is starting out with a gas card or a department store card, which are fairly easy to get. If these two options are not viable, then this third option is the best option for establishing credit, and this is how I started out with my credit. Certain banks offer secured credit cards. A secured credit card works as follows. An individual takes an x amount of dollars and puts it in a savings account. The money that is put in the savings account is secured against the credit that is extended by the bank to the individual. For example, if the individual put $300 in the savings account, the bank would extend credit in the sum of $300.

Let's assume that you received your secured card; now what? What is the best way to build credit? Here are a few steps that are going to make building credit a breeze.

Step one: You should purchase a product or service up to one-third of your credit limit. So if you had a three-hundred-dollar credit line, you should spend one hundred.

Step two: When you receive your bill, pay it off. Pay off that hundred dollars that you used your credit card to purchase a product or service.

Step Three: Repeat step one.

Step Four: This time around, when you receive your

credit card bill, just pay half the bill. In our case, you would pay only fifty dollars of your bill and not the full one hundred dollars.

Step Five: Don't purchase anything; wait until you receive the next credit card bill in the mail.

Step six: Once you receive your new credit card bill, you will notice your fifty-dollar balance plus interest. This time around, pay off the remaining balance and bring it to zero.

Step seven: Repeat steps one through six!

When you do these steps, you are showing creditors that you are a responsible borrower by making payments and paying off your obligations at the same time. You are also helping your credit file by establishing a healthy history, which will help increase your FICO score. One key aspect to remember here is that we are not using credit for our daily purchases but as a means to achieve greater goals in life. Following the above steps will help you build credit in a responsible manner and help you achieve the goals that you have set in your life. A tip I always used to give my clients was that individuals should never have more than 2-3 credit cards. When making large purchases, creditors often look for 3-6 trade lines on the credit report (a trade line is an open credit line that was extended by a creditor). Having a car loan is also considered a trade line. A gas card and department store cards are also considered trade lines.

I would like to discuss the dangers of credit and how

to avoid them. Many people fall into the credit trap. What I mean by this is that many people are tricked into spending more than they have. For example, a credit card company might offer you zero percent interest for twelve months so you can make purchases, and then when the twelve months are over, more often than not, you probably won't have the money to pay all the credit card balance, and that is when the credit card companies get you. When you don't pay the full balance within that twelve-month period, the credit card company will charge you interest. This is where the credit card company makes most of their money; they charge in excess of 12% and higher I have seen some credit card companies charge 20% and higher in interest. There are a few steps that you can take to avoid this particular trap. Always make sure you spend what you can afford in your budget. It is common sense. Don't spend more than what you have, thinking the future will be better and that you could afford that expensive watch or purse. Read the fine print and your credit card agreement, and see how much it would really cost you to buy that expensive watch or purse after those twelve months. Ask the credit card company what would happen if you didn't pay the full amount at the end of those twelve months, what penalties would you incur? The best advice I can give is to shop around town to find the best deal and save your money in advance before purchasing something that you know you can't afford.

It is a known fact that the average household credit card balance as of 2011 is about $8,500. That is a staggering amount and very high. The main reason for this is that when people spend money with their credit card, it is far easier for them to spend! When you carry cash, it is harder to spend because as you spend that cash, you notice that your wallet is getting lighter, and you put the brakes on your spending. One way of getting out of debt is getting a credit card or loan that offers a lower interest rate than what you have currently, and transferring the balance to that card or paying off the credit card with that loan. When you do that, you are lowering your credit card payments and have a fixed payment to make. I usually recommend people take out personal loans or fixed home equity loans, which usually have lower interest rates than credit cards. When you do that, you lower your payments, and it is easier to incorporate these payments into your household or individual budgets.

Credit cards have many benefits as well. Credit cards offer rewards, and there is a growing trend where people make their daily purchases and pay their mortgages with credit cards so that they can take advantage of the many rewards programs that credit card companies have to offer. That is a great idea, but as humans, we tend to overpurchase. In reality, this idea is a great idea, and it could work, but an individual has to be extremely careful and make sure they pay all credit card bills on time and in full in order to avoid all finance charges and penalties that may result from a missed payment or partial payment. Another thing to keep in mind is that when credit cards offer rewards, they have to increase the premium of using the credit card to the merchant; therefore, those premiums are passed through from consumers to the merchants.

Credit Bureaus are the institutions that determine your FICO score. There are three main bureaus: Equifax, Trans Union, and Experian. Banks and lending institutions use these credit bureaus to look at an individual's creditworthiness based on their FICO scores. These three credit bureaus hold great power over our lives and have been subject to many controversies and data breaches over the years. Oftentimes, they engage in unfair practices and ruin people's credit history without a doubt. They don't care about your personal circumstances when they determine your credit, and they often take the financial institution's side when reporting adverse credit inquiries. If an individual wants to dispute an issue he or she has with a financial institution, they would have to go through a cumbersome process and might never get it resolved because of the way their system is designed. I have a lot of criticism about the way the FICO scores are determined and how people's lives get ruined. My biggest gripe with the credit bureaus is that when an individual misses a payment, their credit score is affected adversely immediately, but when an individual pays off a debt or makes payments on time, then it takes the bureaus "forever" to reflect that on an individual's FICO score. I was always told that the credit bureaus are fair, but they are not, and this is a prime example. One excuse I get is that the information is not received fast enough. I call BS! Excuse my language, because when the banks report adversely, it is conveniently received fast enough. I believe that the credit bureaus must go through major reforms because of their unfair practices and the influence they have on people's lives. They are harming people's lives more than helping them. I feel that the bureaus are more favorable towards the financial institution than they are towards individuals, which is not fair at all!

In conclusion, Credit is a great tool if we know how to use it wisely, and I hope I have provided some guidance in this chapter as to how we should use credit and how not to fall into the traps credit cards have. If you follow the formulas in this chapter, I truly believe that you could be successful in managing your money and credit in a wise and responsible manner, where you could use credit as a powerful tool to achieve your goals and dreams.

Ready to start your credit-building journey? Be sure to take advantage of the resources that are available to help you get started. Did you know that once a year, you can download your full credit report from all three bureaus for free? Visit www.freeannualcreditreport.com to get started.

Once you download your credit report, you will know exactly what areas of your credit need attention.

CASH FLOW IS KING

This chapter is the inspiration for the whole book. This is why I decided to write a book about banking. In this chapter, I will be talking about personal finance, how to use your bank accounts to your advantage, and how to make the bank work for you instead of your hard-earned money working for the bank. I will show you how to make a basic budget and how to manage your cash flow within your accounts. I will also introduce you to the concepts of having a fixed expense account and a variable expense account. I will also show you how to avoid overdraft fees that could cost you a small fortune. I will also explain how you could even save some money in this whole process. I only ask that you always remember one basic concept throughout this chapter, and that is what I am about to share with you is what the wealthy use and people with good money management sense use. And it might seem weird in the beginning, but as I explain the concepts and the way the accounts work, it will fit perfectly with the same way, the pieces of a puzzle fit together in a puzzle. I called this chapter Cash flow is king because it is not about how much money you make, it is about how you manage your money! If you, as an individual, realize this aspect of money and that money is a tool for you to reach an end, then accumulating money should not be an issue.

Budgeting is essential, and in my opinion, it is a huge key to anybody's financial success. I will explain how a basic budget works. Every individual has their own circumstances, so I hope you understand that this is a generalized budget, and some people might have more complicated budgets, but for our purposes, I will keep it simple. There are many books and materials out there that explain budgeting in much greater detail. I am sure there are many people who are asking why he has to tell us about budgeting. Well, while I was working in the bank, I came across many people who didn't know what a budget was. I am sure many people have some sort of budget in their head, but in reality, they have no idea that it is called budgeting. I think that budgeting is an essential part of life, and it is unfortunate that our educational system does not teach our young people how to budget.

A budget is very easy to create. A basic budget

shouldn't take more than 20-30 minutes. The way a budget works is basically one's net income every month compared to one's expenses every month. So, what an individual or a household would do is basically get a piece of paper and write down how much income they receive on a monthly basis, and in the other column write their expenses. You then add your expenses and subtract them from your net monthly income. If you get a positive figure, then you're in good shape; if you don't, then you are spending beyond your means. Below is an illustration of a simple budget I created. You can download sophisticated budgets from online or create one yourself in Excel.

Income	Expense
Insert Net income here.	Insert Expenses Here
Example: 2000/mo.	Example: car payment 200/mo
	Rent 1000/mo
	Insurance 100/mo

So, to explain this budget briefly, you take your 2000/mo. Net income and subtract it from your total monthly expenses: 200+1000+100=1300. In our case, we have $700 in positive income every month, which is considered disposable income. It is advisable that when you do your budget that you categorize your expenses by fixed and variable expenses, which takes us to our next subject of fixed and variable accounts.

Many people, especially the young, are used to having one account. We have all grown with the idea that one account is all we need to manage our money. Therefore, many people combine everything into one account; they put their earnings into one account, and they pay all their expenses out of the same account. The problem with this system is that people never seem to keep track of their finances, and they get in trouble by overdrawing their accounts and not keeping track of their budgets. Since I saw this in my banking career, I came out with a formula to help folks with their bank accounts, where they would be able to handle their bank accounts in a more efficient and useful manner. The concept I am about to share might sound weird, but I am asking that we all think outside the box and understand that this concept is proven to work, and I have helped hundreds of people get back on track with their finances, and most importantly, avoid overdraft fees. I am also going to illustrate this concept by presenting an illustration of this formula as well.

As I said before, we are used to having one bank account, but what if I told you that you should have two checking accounts and two savings accounts? You would probably ask me why. Well, here is why. When we separate our accounts into two categories, it would be easier for us to manage our expenses and savings. So, one account would be our fixed expense account, and the other would be our variable expense account. Our fixed expense account would include Rent or mortgage, car payment, insurance, and so forth. Our

Variable expenses would include groceries, gas, going out with friends, etc. On the same token, we would have two separate savings accounts, one for a goal that we are saving for, like a car, house, business, retirement, etc. The second savings account should be used as your emergency fund because you never know when you're going to need it, and trust me when I say you will need those funds one day because everyone has emergency situations. Most banks give you the ability to nickname your accounts online; therefore, I highly advise everyone to nickname each account.

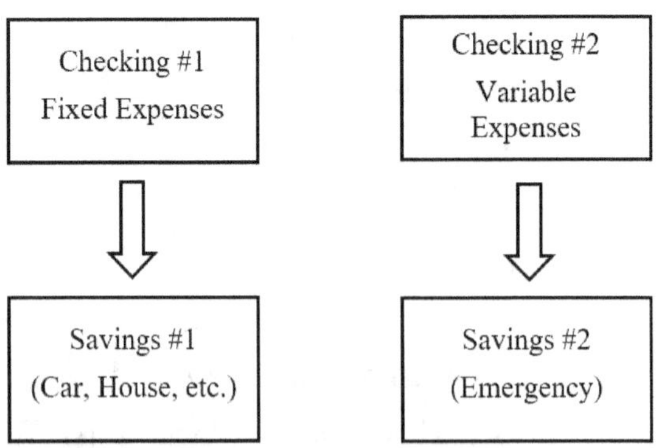

Now that we understand the concept of the fixed and variable expense accounts, we will explain how this formula would work. It is also advisable that you call all your creditors and everyone that you know that you have to pay the same amount every month and have the same due date for all these creditors. This will help tremendously in your cash flow, and it will also help you follow your budget. Therefore, when you get paid, make sure you deposit all the funds into your fixed expense account. Once you do that, pay all of your creditors at once. It is also important that you set up an automatic transfer from your checking account to your savings account. It should be for any amount you feel comfortable with. You should consider yourself as a bill, so when you do your budget, include yourself as an expense. We all know that as your own individual, you are more important than your electrical bill or car insurance, therefore, get yourself in the mindset of treating yourself as an expense. Whatever you have left, you would transfer to your variable expense account. Since you did that, you now know exactly how much money you have left to spend on your variable expenses.

Therefore, you can never overdraw your fixed expense account and incur overdraft fees, and since you transferred the remaining balance to your variable expense account, it is unlikely that you will overdraw your variable expense account. If at the end of the month you have any money left in your variable expense account, then you can go ahead and transfer those funds to any of the savings accounts you feel you would like to save those funds.

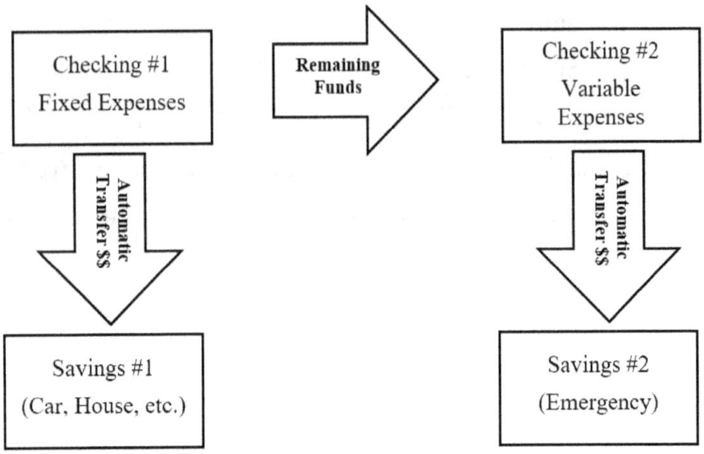

I always tell people that as they progress through life, they should add accounts for other purposes as well. For example, if you have a child, you should maintain an account for your child's expenses and savings as well. When people get married, they should have their own separate accounts and also joint accounts to handle their household expenses and individual expenses. I could go on and on about the type of accounts you should have, but every individual is different, and I believe I gave you the formula to successfully handle your accounts. All you have to do now is use my formula and customize it to your own situation.

A major income stream for the banks is overdraft fees. Banks love charging customers overdraft fees. With the above formula, you shouldn't experience overdraft fees, and you should be able to follow your budget in a more consistent and organized manner. However, there are some situations in which you will fall victim to overdraft fees, and the best way to avoid them is to never opt in to the debit card option, where the bank will pay your debit card transaction even if you don't have the funds available in your account. Banks also offer text and email alerts warning you when you are close to overdrawing your account. You could also set up your own alerts to let you know you reached a certain balance in your account. A rule to abide by is that it is better for your debit card to get declined and you won't be able to pay for that particular transaction than to fall into a cycle of fees that would cost you more than what that transaction is worth. Trust me, banks have no mercy when it comes to overdraft fees.

Another trap is when you write a check and the bank decides to pay that check. That might sound weird, but it is true in some instances, even if you don't have enough funds in your account, the bank might decide to pay that check and charge you a fee. Therefore, I always tell people to follow their budget, manage their cash flow, and never spend beyond their means. If you use these basic principles, then you shouldn't have issues with overdraft fees, and in addition to these principles, following my formula will also help avoid overdraft fees. And I know many people who have used it. These people kept falling victim to the vicious cycle of overdraft fees, and by adjusting a few issues in their financial life (such as not spending beyond their means), and following my formula, they understood that it is truly not about how much money a person makes, but how one manages the funds he/she has. Therefore, my friends, that's why cash flow is king!

Take a moment to review your current spending habits. Download your most recent bank statements and then assess if you need to open separate accounts in order to better manage your funds. Where is the majority of your money going?

On average, how much are you paying in overdraft fees?

How much are you saving?

Needs analysis and net worth calculator

HOW TO CHOOSE THE RIGHT BANK FOR YOU

We all know that every individual is different, and every individual has different tastes and preferences. Therefore, that individual should also choose their bank based on those preferences. In this chapter, I will be discussing how an individual should choose the right bank that is going to be right for him/her.

Traditionally, we always picture the bank as a brick-and-mortar building with tellers and bankers in it. However, with the ever-changing technological advancements, we have seen banks that operate solely online. While working at such banks, both brick-and-mortar and online banks, I found that it is really important for people to know how to choose the right bank. What I mean by this is that many people were attracted to the fact that online banks offer better rates on their savings accounts because their overhead is much lower than traditional banks, but they had a hard time grasping concepts such as electronic fund transfers, aka EFT (EFT is when someone transfers funds electronically), or linking their checking account at their traditional bank to their virtual savings account. Therefore, when you choose a bank, make sure you are comfortable with the way the bank does business and their business model. Make sure you ask your banker how their bank operates. Make sure that the bank's ease of use matches your preferences and that you are comfortable with the way they do business. It is important that you do your research about how your bank operates, which is readily available online, or you could ask any branch manager, and they'll be more than happy to help and share information with you. I know that many people have the mindset of rate shopping for the bank that they choose, but that doesn't always translate to good service or ease of use, and oftentimes, I've seen people leave banks that offer higher rates and come back to their old bank because the bank's business model didn't match their needs and preferences.

Now that we know that ease of use and the bank's business model are important aspects in choosing a bank, the next step has to be customer service. When doing business at the bank, it is often a pleasant experience. Most people like going to the bank because they encounter friendly staff who are knowledgeable as well. People believe it or not, while standing in line, interact with each other while waiting to be served. I highly recommend that you listen to the conversations people have been in line because more often than not, they are talking about the service they are receiving from the bank, and that is a good indication of how you will be treated. Therefore, when you look for a bank, make sure that the bank you choose has high standards for customer service. Another way you could find out if a bank places a high regard for customer service is by finding out how happy the employees working at the bank are. Finding this information is quite easy. What you want to do is ask about employee turnover. If employees quit or get fired often, then that should be a red flag for poor service. The reason is that the bank is not hiring the right people to service the customers it has, and it is not treating its employees right; therefore, those employees won't provide the best service possible. Over the years, big traditional banks have failed in providing adequate customer service to their customers; therefore, they have implemented surveys by Gallup to get a sense of where they can improve when it comes to customer service. However, we must understand that service in any industry is abstract. It is never a clean cut to the point concept or issue that has defined guidelines. The reason is that the people who walk into the bank have different personalities, and it is impossible to adapt a clear-cut way to handle people; therefore, banks do the best they can to accommodate their customers.

Another concept of choosing a bank is the convenience factor. When you choose a bank, you must feel comfortable reaching the bank and having access to the bank. When I would talk to people about this, they never gave bank convenience great importance, but when events happened to them after I spoke to them, often they would thank me for making them open an account at the bank I was working at. It is my opinion that every single individual should have an account at a major national bank that has plenty of locations domestically or overseas. There are several benefits, the most important one is when you travel and you need cash, it is good to know that you have access to your money since there is a local branch of your account. Another benefit of having the convenience of branches is that when you need to make business transactions, you can walk into a branch and conduct your business. I also know that many people might think that having access to branches is no longer important because of the internet, but this is where they are wrong. Often times people travel, and in some cases, they encounter an emergency, and knowing that they can walk into a branch and talk to someone face to face gives them peace of mind. Convenience is also important when it comes to the bank's accessibility to your funds. What this means is that we all need cash at some point or another. Having access to ATM's when banks are closed is a major aspect customers should look at. Therefore, I always recommend you choose a bank that has many ATM locations, especially when we know that banks charge hefty fees for using other banks ATM's. Another important aspect is that you should look for a bank that offers a debit card. A debit card is a convenient way of shopping and conducting business. The way a debit card works is exactly the same as a credit card; the only difference is that when you use the debit card, funds are deducted from your checking account. Also, some debit cards offer rewards depending on the bank, but that may require an additional annual fee.

When choosing a bank, it ultimately comes down to your preferences. If you feel comfortable with your bank and you like the staff, along with the bank's policies and procedures, then you have found the right bank for you. I am sure there are many other factors that dictate the way you would choose your bank, and that has to do with personal preference. What I have done in this chapter is to make you aware of some important aspects that you should look out for when choosing the right bank for you.

Now I would like to delve into banks' products and services. Banks offer many products and services, and navigating through the maze of these products and services could be really hard and, in many cases, confusing as well. Therefore, I decided to "go there," so to speak, and make people's lives a bit easier by trying to explain these products and services. I will be concentrating on the most popular products and services and if you need more info about a product not mentioned in this book I urge you to speak with your banker. Chapter ten will explain in greater detail, some of the products offered by banks.

Banks make money by taking in deposits and lending money against the deposits made, like we discussed in chapter one. In order to do this, the bank has to offer vehicles to accept people's money so it can lend that money to the general public. Some of these vehicles are checking, savings, and certificate of deposit accounts, aka CDs. Checking accounts are accounts usually used for paying bills and used as an expense account where money comes in and we use that money to pay our day-to-day expenses. The checking account usually comes with a checkbook and a debit card. Today, checking account balances and activity may be viewed online, and most banks offer online bill pay, where customers can pay their bills online without using a checkbook. Another aspect of the checking account is that it is extremely liquid, and it gives the account owner access to his/her money at any given time.

Then there is the savings account. This is a type of account where people usually save money for a goal that they have in mind. This account earns interest as well and has the benefit of compound interest. Compound interest is when interest is added to the principal, and you will be earning interest on the new principal amount. There are certain rules that apply to savings accounts that will be covered in Chapter Ten.

Savings accounts are also considered liquid accounts,

where one has access to their account at any given time. However, with a savings account, it is really important to know that you can only withdraw six times a month from it. If you exceed that amount and withdraw more than six times, you will get penalized with a fee, and if you continue withdrawing more than six times a month, the bank will close your savings account. I have seen it happen many times, and I have seen bank customers get really frustrated about it, but I have told them that it is a federal requirement and the bank has no say in it. The reason why you could withdraw only six times a month from a savings account is very simple. It is because a savings account is meant to be a savings account, so any money that goes into that account is meant to stay there. So, by limiting the amount of withdrawals, the government thinks people are more likely to save.

The next basic bank product that most people are familiar with is the certificate of deposit, or CD for short. The CD is a savings vehicle that you would put a sum of money into and receive an interest rate that is fixed for a certain period of time. Usually, a CD has a higher interest rate than a savings account, and the funds are not accessible until the CD matures. Once the CD matures, you have a choice of withdrawing the money and closing the account with the interest that you earned, of course, or you could just let the CD roll over to the same duration, but in most cases, you will receive a new rate based on the current market rates. If you let the CD roll over, you will have a new principal balance since the interest you earned is now part of the principle. When this happens, if you decide to roll over the CD, you can take advantage of the principle of compound interest. However, if you decide to close the CD, you can choose another CD with different terms or just put it into your savings account, or decide to do something else with the funds; it is entirely up to you. All the accounts mentioned above are insured by the FDIC, an agency governed by the government of the United States.

Another bank product is the investment accounts. The most notable ones are mutual funds. To get into this type of account, you will have to talk to a specialized licensed banker. These accounts carry risks and are not guaranteed by the bank or the FDIC; therefore, it is highly advisable that you do your homework before you open an account of this type.

I will be going into more details about the types of accounts bank offer and explaining in more detail about the type of accounts banks offer in a later chapter.

3 things the bank doesn't tell you about your account

FDIC accounts and insurance

BANK POLICIES

This Chapter came into being out of necessity. I think that this chapter is necessary because many people out there don't understand bank policies and why they are in place. There is a misconception by many people about the rules and policies banks have, and many people believe and think that the rules and policies banks have are cumbersome and unnecessary. However, I am not here to change people's minds about these policies and rules, and I am certainly not here to be an advocate on behalf of the banks. I am just clarifying to the readers and explaining why these policies were put in place by the banks and what the reasons behind them are. In this chapter, I will be discussing account opening requirements, hold policies, bank fees, and bank limits on accounts and ATM's.

Opening an account might sound like an easy task

where you just walk into a bank and ask for a banker, tell the banker that you want a checking account, and then the banker types in your info and

"Voila," you have an account. Well, that scenario can happen and does happen at times, but that is not the way it should be. Banks require that people show two forms of ID when opening their accounts. This requirement is extremely important because most identity theft occurs at account openings. So, make sure the banker asks for your ID. This bank policy is put in place to protect the customer. The forms of ID acceptable as primary ID are any state or federal ID issued by the government, such as a driver's licenses, state ID, or passport. Acceptable secondary IDs are credit cards and debit cards. Bankers might ask you questions regarding yourself when you open an account they want to get to know you and your needs so they can place you in the right products and services. However, many bankers don't always look out for the best interest of their clients, and they put their clients in the wrong accounts so they receive the most commission or credit. Therefore, I always advise people to go online to the bank's website and read about the account features, requirements, and policies. Major issues to look for are minimum balances, monthly service charges, and the bank's overdraft policies.

The most annoying part of banking is the holds placed on funds deposited into one's account. This is where most people get frustrated. Now, I understand that people have to have access to their funds and that cash flow is of extreme importance; however, one also has to understand the risk associated with checks especially checks that are of large denominations. Therefore, the banks have devised certain guidelines that determine the risk associated with a check. The banks look at several factors. I won't get into all of them because there are many, but I will mention the most important ones. The first factor banks look into is your account history. The bank looks at how long you have had the account with the bank. If you have had an account for a long time, the likelihood of you bailing on the check is low, meaning that you will eventually cover the amount of the check. A second major factor is your average daily balance in your account. When the bank sees a healthy average balance, it knows that you will be able to cover the check in case of a default. Another factor affecting holds and their duration is overdraft fees and bounced checks that you have had. If the bank sees that you have had many checks that have bounced, then that is a red flag for the bank. Another factor that affects the duration of the hold specifically is the location of the bank where the check was drawn. If the branch where the check was drawn is on the East Coast but the depositor is depositing the check on the West Coast, that is a red flag, and the time it takes for the check to clear also increases. These are the most important factors for holds. Now, local checks usually are placed on 2 business day holds. Out-of-state checks could be anywhere from 5-7 business days, sometimes even up to 11 business days. Checks over $5,000 might have longer period holds.

One of the bank's major revenue streams is bank fees. Fees come in different disguises; therefore, Fees are hated by people because they feel that it is just the bank to charge a high fee on an account that has overdrafted. Now, I agree that it is not fair for a bank to charge thirty-five dollars for an overdraft of two dollars from buying coffee at a Starbucks. I really don't agree with those fees. However, it is also a person's responsibility not to overdraw his or her account. Therefore, when you overdraw your account, the bank has the right to penalize you, but it has to be reasonable. I believe that most banks exaggerate the amount of fees they charge. This is why people resent banks. There are some fees that are indeed justified. Charging consumers for checks, cashier's checks, bank checks, and money orders is fair. Charging for people's accounts, I don't feel, is fair because after all, the bank is making money on the money we are storing in their bank. So, when we look at banks and the fees they charge, we have to understand that the bank has to charge these fees to stay in business and to cater to its clientele. After all, banks have major overhead such as brick and mortar buildings, payroll, and maintaining the accounts cost money as well. However, I believe that banks sometimes overcharge people for their services, and this is a major concern that many people have. Although these concerns might be legitimate and rightful, we must understand that banks will continue to charge fees. The amount of fees they will be charging is open to debate, but banks must realize that the days when they were charging high overdraft fees are over, and people must also realize that, in order for banks to stay in business, not all services are free, and they might have to pay a fee for certain services that the bank has to offer.

When someone opens a brand-new account, their account might have limits. You are asking yourself what limits? Well, when you deposit a check into a new account, that check is most likely to go on hold. Like I mentioned before, when you open a new account, the risk to the bank is high; therefore, they put certain limits on your account for the first few months until they get to know you. If you have a new account or are planning to open a new account, don't be surprised if your checks go on hold. However, if you have a good relationship with your banker and your banker knows you, the banker or branch manager could help remove the hold from your deposit and make funds available to you faster.

While working at the bank, I would encounter many people who would want their ATM limits increased. The majority of banks have a three-hundred-dollar limit on ATM withdrawals, and some banks go up to five

hundred dollars. Debit card purchase limits are usually higher. The reason for all these debit card and ATM withdrawal limits is the risk the bank is exposed to. The banks fear that if someone gets a hold of your debit card and pin, then they could withdraw large sums of cash, but when limits are placed, the risk is minimized, and fraud is also minimized. Banks lose a tremendous amount of money due to fraud and electronic theft. Therefore, in my opinion, it is justified that banks put limits not only to protect the bank but also to protect the consumer against fraud and theft. When banks put limitations on certain transactions, even though it might be frustrating at times, it is important to remember that these limitations are placed to protect you, the consumer. It has happened that fraud and theft were prevented because bank guidelines were followed and limitations were placed. From my own personal experience, I had many customers thank me for placing a hold on a check they wrote because their wallet got stolen with their checkbooks in it. So, before you get angry about holds and limits, remember that these safeguards were placed to protect you against fraud and theft.

FDIC, also known as the Federal Deposit Insurance **Corporation**. I underlined the corporation, colored it in red, and made it bold to make a point. "The FDIC is an independent agency of the United States government," based on what it says on its website. They also say that they are in the business of protecting your deposits at a bank in case a bank or savings association fails and goes bankrupt (source: FDIC.gov). They even go further to say that they are "backed by the full faith and credit of the United States government."The FDIC will insure up to $250,000 per depositor. If you go to their website, you could get information on how you could increase deposit amounts, or go to your local bank and talk to a banker about making sure your deposits are insured properly.

The FDIC plays another role as well; it protects our money in case banks fail. The way that FDIC pays you if your bank fails is as follows: If there is a "healthy" bank, which I assume is a bank that is in great financial standing, it can take over the deposits of the failed bank. We saw this happen in 2008 when some banks failed due to the mortgage meltdown, i.e., the Chase takeover of Washington Mutual. If there are no "Healthy" banks to take over deposits then the FDIC will dispense checks directly to the depositors within a few days after the bank closes; however I have read and heard from reliable sources that the FDIC has 99 years to pay out which means that if we had a whole bunch of banks fail then we would be all screwed if the rumor that the FDIC has 99 years to pay out our money.

To conclude, THE FDIC was created after the great depression for people to have faith in the strength of US financial institutions and be confident that what happened during the great depression won't repeat itself. Now, should we trust the FDIC to be there when we really need it? The answer is, would you trust the government with your money? Whatever answer you gave, that is what you should be comfortable with.

BANK ETHICS

This chapter is a crucial chapter, and I really wanted to write about ethics in a bank. As you read this chapter, you might feel that I am anti-consumer, but that is not true at all. I just want to address some issues that will help you, the reader, succeed with your banking experience. While I was working in the bank, I found many people to be rude, obnoxious, and downright out of line. First, I would like to make one thing very clear: a bank is a **professional place of business**! It is in no shape or form a place where you can come and behave like you would if you went to a club or social gathering. I would often see people come to the bank with their pajamas and other inappropriate attire. Even though we live in a free country, I think there should be a certain type of respect when we go to the bank. I would often see people bring their pets to the bank, which I find to be out of line. Don't take me wrong, I love animals, but a bank is not a place for your pet. I had other customers complain about pets more

often than you might think. I do agree that we must allow pets for the disabled and blind, but other than that, pets should not be taken to banks out of respect for other people.

On many occasions, people would be standing in line and complain about the long wait times that they had to endure. People also blame the bank for not having enough tellers open to cater to them. I certainly understand their concern, but I find it baseless! There are several reasons for this. First and foremost, the reason the line is long is because the person standing in front of the teller did not come prepared or is chatting away about how her in-laws are giving her hell, or some other personal issue that has nothing to do with banking. Therefore, before you get upset at the bank employees, you should always say to yourself why the person who was in front of you, who knows that there is a long line, is not prepared and is talking about personal matters when there is a long line. In my opinion, that is rude and a burden on other customers waiting in line to conduct their business. The second reason is when people come during times when everybody seems to come at the same time, like lunch time or after work. If you come to the bank when you know there are going to be many people in the bank wanting to conduct business, then the rule of thumb is to be prepared to wait and not complain. Otherwise, ask the manager or a bank employee what the best times to visit the bank are, based on when the bank is not busy

so that you can avoid the long wait times. I am mentioning this issue because people would get aggravated because they would come to the bank during their lunch times, and they would see a line out the door. I highly recommend that people save themselves the aggravation and not go to the bank during their lunch times if they are not willing to wait in line and wait their turn. I find it really offensive, and I think any logical person would as well, to take out your frustration on a bank employee just because you don't have time to wait in line. If that is the case, please come to the bank at a time that is convenient for you, where you will have time to wait if you have to, and you won't get stressed or aggravated because of the long wait times.

Another issue I would like to address is when people are told of certain bank policies and are aware of them, and they refuse to abide by them, and when a bank employee enforces those policies, they get upset. Banks, over the years, have gotten tougher with their policies and procedures, and it does aggravate many people, and many people feel that they are privileged and deserve special treatment and even some of the rules to bend for them, but when an employee enforces those rules, they get upset and become obnoxious because things didn't go their way. I find that to be rude and offensive, and I have refused to give service to people who have asked me to jeopardize my job in the past, and on many occasions, those people would complain and make false accusations about my service towards them, just because I was following bank policies. Now, I know that I sound harsh, but what I suggest you do is when you come across a situation that is frustrating to you in the bank, it is important to remember to always talk with respect and try not to lose your cool, be nice and calm. Also, if you remember in a previous chapter when I wrote about how important relationships with your banker are, I mentioned that bankers can help you navigate through banks' policies and procedures. Therefore, if you feel frustrated or mad, talk to your banker and see if he or she can help with your issue.

I want to share with you a personal experience that I went through at the bank while standing in line, and I want to know if it was appropriate for a customer to engage in the behavior she did. Before I continue, I want to say that I was not a bank employee when this happened, but I was a regular bank customer waiting my turn like every other bank customer. While waiting in line, a middle-aged lady walks into the bank, and the line happens to be long. There were three tellers open, and they were all helping customers with their transactions. The bank manager was in the lobby, greeting customers and answering customers' questions. The assistant bank manager was also trying to help to the best of her ability. This particular lady started to make comments such as I am in a hurry, I am parked at the meter, and the time is going to run out. Now the bank has free parking for bank patrons, why in the world wouldn't she park in the bank parking? She started complaining and getting louder and louder about the service and how she doesn't have time to wait. The bank manager told this particular lady that he would go and put quarters in the meter just to appease her. Now, while I was standing in line, I noticed that the customers at the teller window were not prepared or were asking the teller a million questions. Now I feel that customers have all the right in the world to ask questions and do their business; however, it is not always the teller or the bank's fault. You have to wait in line for a long time, in many cases, more often than you would think, the fault lies with the customer. Now, this lady was really rude, and I found her to be lazy and just someone who is spoiled. She could have parked in the bank's parking lot and avoided the stress she went through, or she could have left and come at a different time when she had more time. Instead, she took out her frustrations on the bank and was vocal about it and making it unpleasant for the other customers and herself.

I am going to give one last example of rudeness by customers at the bank. That is when the bank teller or banker asks for an ID, and for whatever reason, you don't have an ID to prove you are the person asking to do a bank transaction. Now, many people get offended and say, "I've been banking at this bank for the past thirty years, you would think you guys would know me by now". This is only one of many comments people make. Well, it is true that you might have been banking at the same branch for many years; however, banks have systems and software that require your driver's license or ID number to be inputted before the teller or banker can proceed to the next stage of the transaction. I am sure you don't expect the teller or banker to remember every single driver's license number, right? It is possible that you might see tellers or bankers who have been working at the same branch for many years, and they probably know you very well, and you have established good, solid relationships with those individuals; however, they would still need to see your ID in order to help you with your transaction. Furthermore, people should be happy that their bank is making sure that only they have access to your account and that the bank is doing whatever is in its power to protect their account from fraud and identity theft. Also, arguing with the teller and banker just prolongs your transaction and creates inconvenience for other people waiting to get their business done. To end this, I would like to give a word of advice: next time you go to the bank, thank the teller or banker for asking for your ID and tell them that you appreciate them taking the necessary steps to protect your money and your account. This will make the teller and banker feel good about themselves, and in some cases, they would go out of their way to accommodate you if you ever need their help for any particular transaction.

To end this chapter, I would like to give you some words of advice when going to the bank. Don't go to the bank if you are in a bad mood. Don't go to the bank if you are in a hurry, because you might get upset for waiting in line or not being able to make it to your doctor's appointment, for example. On many occasions, if you need to see your banker, you can call him or her and make an appointment at a set time and see him or her to take care of your business; this way, if you are in a hurry, you won't have to stress because you know your banker will be available to help you. However, when it comes to the teller line, that is not the case; therefore, inquire with a banker or a manager when the slow times occur during branch hours where traffic is slow, so you can have no wait or minimal wait times. Don't go to the bank if you think you are upset at the bank, and you think that by taking your frustration out on the first person you see, it will help resolve your issue, because it won't; it will only make matters worse. Lastly, always remember that the bank is a place of business, and there is no reason to be rude or think that the people who work there are your servants. Always treat the bank employees with respect and give them acknowledgment for the job they are doing. I know that many people in today's economy are frustrated with the banks, and they feel that banks are making a ton of money on people's expense, which is open for debate.

However, taking out your anger on the bank employees is no the way of solving your issues that you might have, therefore, as discussed before, having a solid relationship with a banker and the branch manager is key to solving banking issues and having a more relaxed and pleasant banking experience.

HOW LOANS WORK

I am excited about this chapter because this is the area of my expertise. I worked in the mortgage business for a few years, and what I loved about the loan business is that every day I would learn something new. I will start by explaining a few loan products and what their functions are, what they should be used for, and how they can help you reach your financial goals. Loans are not a simple matter to explain; therefore, I will be explaining how various loans work and how banks and financial institutions choose who to lend to and who not to lend to, and what criteria they choose in determining who they lend to, known as underwriting. Underwriting is the process by which lenders determine who they lend to, based on criteria they have established. I would also like to share my opinion on the way credit scores are determined and the fallacies of credit rating agencies in their credit scoring process. Finally, I will discuss the loan process, closing the loan, repaying the loan, and the consequences of not paying your loan, and how to deal with it.

The first type of loan I'd like to start with is called the starter loan. This is a loan that almost everyone gets approved for when they start their adult life, and that is a department store card or a gas card to be used at gas stations. Some examples are Sears, Macy's card, or a Shell or Chevron gas card. These cards are very good to use as getaway card to build your credit, and following what I wrote in the previous chapter about building credit and how to build credit. These are cards that will open the door for bigger loans, which takes us to the next type of loan: credit cards.

Credit cards are called the devil's loan in my opinion because these loans have trapped many people and ruined many good people's financial lives. A credit card lets people purchase items or services and allows people to make payments on their credit card with an interest rate determined by the financial institution. The rates banks charge on credit cards is outrageous and out of control, and many people are lured into using credit cards because of the financial institutions' lure of benefits ranging from travel points all the way to cash rewards. It is important to understand that in return for all these so-called rewards, the financial institution will be charging you a higher interest rate. People often fall for credit cards and are careless, and I think it is normal human nature. By nature, people like things, and when financial institutions extend credit to people, they play on people's nature, because people will always spend more than they can afford, and in my humble opinion, financial institutions have done a great job exploiting human nature and trapping many people in their trap, and have ruined many lives. It is extremely important to understand that credit should be used in a responsible and disciplined manner. A person should never spend more than he or she can afford. Therefore, I can't stress enough how important it is to understand that credit should be used to advance a person's life and build personal wealth, and not the wealth of the banks. As you may recall, in a previous chapter, I mentioned how one should use credit cards to build credit in a responsible manner. I highly recommend that you go back and read that chapter if you have forgotten the information.

The next loan that most people are familiar with is the personal loan. This type of loan is more advanced, as it requires a person to have an established credit history and a steady income. Today, we see many ads on TV offering people personal loans regardless of their credit, as long as they have a job. These loans can carry high interest rates and could, in some cases, be worse than credit cards. Personal loans carry a revolving line of credit; therefore, every time you pay off the loan, you can tap into that credit line and use it for whatever reason you would like. A personal loan usually carries a high interest rate because these loans are riskier for banks since there is no collateral to back them up. Personal loans are usually used to consolidate other loans, such as credit cards, into one convenient payment.

The next type of loan is the auto loan. Auto loans are financed by dealerships, banks, credit unions, and consumer credit institutions. The Auto loan is almost always granted as long as an individual has a job and a bank account. When a person has good credit, it helps them get better terms for the loan, where they don't have to pay high interest rates; therefore, granting them lower monthly payments. The auto loan is also a great way for people to start building their credit, and many lenders like to see a good history of payments with auto loans, because it shows them that you are responsible with making payments on a large purchase; therefore, you are more likely to be responsible with your home loan as well. Auto loans are different than leases because they grant title and ownership to the car after the term of the loan. Leasing a car does not grant ownership to the car, and you either have to trade in the car and get a new lease or take out a new auto loan to finance the purchase of the car. In most cases, auto dealers will deduct the lease payment you have made and reduce it from the cost of the purchase price, giving you a lower loan amount for the purchase of the car. Purchasing RVs and boats similar guidelines and characteristics.

The next type of loan would be the student loan.

Student loans are usually given to people who are attending a college or university. To qualify for student loans, you must be enrolled in an accredited college approved by the federal government. Many people use student loans as a complement to financial aid. The way this would work is, let's assume that you are a college student and you apply for financial aid. Let's say that you qualify for X amount of money; however, the tuition for your school for the year, semester, or quarter far exceeds that of what you got in financial aidand/and grants. Therefore, you would apply through the same application (FAFSA application) for a student loan. The application would be forwarded to the Federal government, and you would get a loan for x amount of dollars to pay for your tuition, books, and living expenses; or let's assume you don't qualify for financial aid and you can't afford to pay the tuition out of pocket, then you would apply for a student loan. The requirements for a student loan are set by the federal government, and the benefits are that you get lower interest rates, you can start paying off your loan after you complete your education, and you can refinance your loan if lower rates are available. In some instances, there are no credit requirements to get this type of financing. The way banks get involved in this process is that after the federal government approves these loans, the servicing of the loans becomes the bank's responsibility. The federal government guarantees these loans the same way Fannie Mae and Freddie Mac do mortgages (I will discuss these two corporations' roles shortly). Getting a student loan is a great way to further someone's education. In today's rising market of tuition rates and the ever-competitive job market, many people are going back to school to further their education and have a competitive advantage. That is why student loans are really important in our economy, because it is a way for the economy to move forward and for our country to be on the cutting edge of innovation. Plus, it opens up many venues and opportunities for people all throughout this country. The disadvantages of a student loan are that you must pay it back! Unlike any other loan, student loans must be repaid even if you are going through economic turmoil. Bankruptcy does not discharge you from paying your student loans, and you must keep making your payments. However, you can, in some cases, ask your lender to extend you forbearance for a period of time until your situation improves. If you need to get more information regarding student loans, I highly recommend that you talk to your admissions office on your campus or your financial aid office to get full details on how student loans work for your particular situation.

Mortgage loans are among my favorites to discuss. The reason I like this subject is that I worked in this industry and I am passionate about it. When you work in this industry, you learn something new every single day. It is also rewarding knowing that you have genuinely helped an individual achieve their dream of home ownership. I am going to admit it is hard for me to write this section because there is so much I can write about; however, I have decided that I am going to make this section as generalized as possible because there is so much information out there about home mortgages. I am going to touch on the most important aspect of mortgages so that people are knowledgeable when they apply for a mortgage and can carry on an intelligent and fruitful conversation with their loan officers and brokers. There are several ways of attaining a home mortgage. A person can choose to walk into a bank and start a conversation with the loan officer or apply for a loan online. People also look for different home loans through mortgage brokers or bankers. Later, I will also discuss the differences between each of these individuals so that you can make an informed decision about how you should apply for a home loan. However, I am going to talk about the different types of home loans first. I am going to start with fixed loans, and the most popular loan in the fixed loan category is the 30-year fixed loan. This means that the rate of the loan would be fixed for 30 years and amortized over 30 years. This type of loan is for People who are planning on staying at their residence for a long period of time.

The next loan that is a popular fixed-rate mortgage is the 15-year fixed-rate mortgage, which is amortized over 15 years. The fifteen-year fixed mortgage will have a higher payment amount, but it affords the borrower the luxury of paying the loan off in a much more accelerated manner. This loan, as a thirty-year fixed mortgage, is great for people who are considering a residence for a long period of time and want to pay off their loan faster.

I am now going to get into the adjustable-rate mortgages, aka ARM loans, and what they are. An adjustable-rate mortgage means that the rate would be fixed for a certain amount of time, and after that fixed period, the rate would adjust based on an index (usually the prime rate).

The types of loans mostly associated with ARMare the 1/1, 3/1, 5/1, 7/1, and 10/1. Now you might be wondering what these numbers mean, so please allow me to clarify. Let's use the 5/1 ARM loan as an example. The first digit 5 means that the rate would be fixed for the first five years, but it would be motorized for 30 years. After the 5 years are over, the rate would adjust according to the index it is tied to for the remainder of the life of the loan. However, the rate would adjust annually, and that is what the 1 represents. This type of loan traditionally offers a lower rate and is great for first-time home buyers and for people who do not intend to stay in their house for a long period of time. Statistics have shown that people usually move every five to seven years, which makes these types of loans very attractive. Another reason people like this loan is that they anticipate a raise in their income, so when they are faced with a rate increase, they can deal with it. Another advantage of this type of loan is that, because it offers a lower rate than the fixed rate loans, it is only when the markets offer lower rates that you could take advantage of that situation and allow the rate to adjust, and in most cases, your rate would be lower than what the markets have to offer if you were to refinance. However, there is a risk that most people fear, and that is when the rates adjust, they would be facing a higher rate, thus having to make higher payments. My recommendation is to always consider the time you are planning on staying in the property and what your income is going to be in the future. Adjustable-rate mortgages do have caps, meaning that once the loan term passes the fixed rate period, it will not increase above that cap. Different lenders have different types of caps. The most popular caps are 2/2/6 and 5/2/5. These caps are in place to provide a safety net for the borrower, so the shock of the rate increase will be manageable for the borrower to pay the monthly mortgage payment.

I would like to mention that all the loans that I mentioned above have an interest-only option, which means that an individual would only pay the interest portion of the loan, and none of the payments would go towards the principal. The duration of the interest-only option is usually for the first ten years. I would also like to point out that the shorter the loan term, the lower the interest rate; however, there are some instances based on the bond market and the secondary markets where you will have slightly higher rates on shorter-term loans, but that rarely occurs.

The next loan I would like to talk about is hard money loans. Hard money loans are usually used for "flipping" houses, which means that an investor would buy a property that needs renovations done to it, so the investor would take out a hard money loan that would consider the future value of the property, and based on that, the investor would receive the loan amount. The investor would then renovate the property and turn around and sell it. To qualify for this loan is fairly simple; it depends on the value and equity of the property. It does not take into consideration any credit or income considerations like traditional loans do. The cost of these loans is very high, and they always have a higher interest rate than traditional loans. Hard money loans are also very dangerous because a default on the payment means imminent foreclosure. I say this because the interest rates on hard money loans are higher than standard loans, and the likelihood of default is higher as well.

Hard money loans are also known as "flipping loans." Many investors who buy homes that need rehabilitation use these loans to fund their purchase and rehab the property and turn around and sell the house for a profit and pay off the hard money loan in the process. Guidelines for hard money loans usually require a 20%-30% down payment or equity.

The next topic in loans, we are going to talk about business loans and how they help business owners with their daily operations. I will also delve into the various types of business loans available and explain the requirements for applying to them, as well as their purpose.

The process of getting a business loan requires a business owner to apply for the loan through a bank or a non-bank lender. Part of the application process requires documentation submitted by the business owner for the underwriter to see if the business owner is qualified to receive the loan. Several documents might be required by banks, such as contracts with suppliers, agreements the business owner entered into or any credit obligation the business owner defaulted on or is paying on time. Collateral is another determinant. Depending on the type of loan the business owner is applying for, the lender may require collateral to secure financing. The business owner's reputation could also play a role in obtaining a business loan from a bank. If a business owner has a relationship with the bank and has a business account, and has a history of continuous deposits and business transactions,it greatly increases the business owner's chances of receiving a business loan. The longer the relationship with the bank, the greater the odds are to receiving a loan.

Credit scores are a major way a lender determines a business owner's eligibility for a business loan. Different lenders have different FICO score requirements. Obviously, the higher the business owner's score, the more favorable loan terms the business owner will receive. I would like to mention that lenders would also look at the business credit, which is determined by Dun & Bradstreet.

When applying for a business loan, the lender will always pull credit.

Tax returns and profit, bank statements, and profit and loss documents are a major determinant regarding whether a business owner would get a business loan because they would show the business owner's financial strength in paying back the loan.

I would like to mention that you have two main players in the business loan arena: the traditional banks and online banks. The difference between these banks is that the traditional banks will take longer to fund your business loan and will have a more personal touch to it, whereas an online bank has predetermined algorithms to determine whether or not the business owner is worthy to get a loan. The process with online lenders is much faster and, in some cases, easier to obtain a loan through them.

Now let's get into the different types of business loans and what is needed to apply to them, and what their purpose is.

1. Long-term loans: These business loans typically have a duration of 10 years, which serves the purpose of a business owner to pay off the loan over a 10-year period. This business loan is for the purpose of paying off a large investment. Here is a list of typical documents needed depending on the amount of the loan the business owner is asking for:

a. Tax returns.
b. Profit and Loss Statements.
c. Balance Sheet.
d. Business Debt Schedule.
e. Business plan.

2. Short-term loans: The purpose of this business loan is to cover unexpected expenses, infuse cash for business growth, or to cover any cash flow issues the business might encounter. The length of these loans is usually about 18 months or a year and a half. Rates on short-term business loans are higher. Here are some of the documents that you might need:

a. Tax returns.
b. Balance sheet.
c. Cash flow projections.
d. Business account statements.
e. Business license, where applicable.
f. Business Plan.

3. Merchant cash advance loans: This is a loan that is based on the business owner's credit card processing transactions. The lender will use the credit card processing data from the past month or two and lend based on the volume of credit card transactions. The lender will, in return, receive payment of future credit

card transactions at a premium. Usually used for cash flow issues. Here are some of the documents that you need:

a. Merchant processing statement (credit card processing statement).
b. Business account statements.
c. Tax ID Number.

4. Business lines of credit: This is a loan that is usually used to help business owners with working capital issues, cash flow issues, equipment repairs, purchase of inventory, equipment, and other items that business owners might need. There are two categories that fall under this type of loan: an unsecured business line of credit or an unsecured business line of credit. An unsecured line of credit would require the business owner to provide a personal guarantee. Their personal credit profile is a strong indication of whether they will receive it or not. A secured business line of credit would require the business owner to offer some sort of collateral, such as equipment or some other asset. Here are some of the documents necessary for this type of loan:

a. Tax returns.
b. Business bank statements.
c. Business license.
d. Profit and loss statement.

e. Cash flow statements.
f. Personal bank statements with personal tax documents.

5. Account receivable financing, AKA invoice financing: First, let's explain what accounts receivable mean. It means essentially refers to what other businesses or individuals owe the business and is still outstanding. Therefore, a business owner may use these receivables as collateral to get a business loan. The business lender would use these receivables to determine a value and, in turn, determine the loan amount or line of credit amount. Some documents that might be needed:

a. Tax returns.
b. Some invoices.
c. Credit report.
d. Your business entity documentation, i.e., DBA, LLC, INC.
e. Your accounts payable and receivable.

6. Equipment Financing: This is a loan used to purchase equipment used during the course of the business, such as a truck, computers, commercial ovens, tables and desks, etc. The equipment is most likely going to be used as collateral as well. The following is what you will need to get this type of loan:

a. Tax returns.
b. Business plan.
c. Your CV or resume.
d. Profit and loss statements.
e. Your credit report.
f. The type of business you are running. i.e., Inc., LLC, DBA.

7. SBA Loans: This type of loan is the most popular loan there is. Requirements for this loan differ based on the type of SBA loan one will get. A business owner would have to apply for this loan through a retail bank or non-bank lenders, such as business loan brokers. The process of obtaining an SBA loan could be lengthy and cumbersome.

Here are my tips on making the business loan process a breeze.

1. Make sure you are organized! Have all of your paperwork ready and presentable. Gather as much paperwork and documentation as possible so that when you apply, you can submit it for faster response times and an underwriting process.

2. Business loan lenders will want to know if you have a plan B just in case you can't pay off your loan due to some unforeseen circumstance. This could help secure the loan, especially if you have other sources of capital or collateral, because the lender would know that revenue is not the only source for paying off the loan.

3. There is a saying, "it's who you know, not what you know," that makes a difference! Therefore, make sure you present a few references when applying for a business loan. References could be vendors, customers, or business partners. References should highlight your success in business and your stellar performance in paying any outstanding debt.

4. Honesty! Make sure you are honest and truthful when you apply for a business loan because if a lender smells anything fishy, the loan is dead in its tracks. You have been warned!

Now that you have a grasp of what business loans are and what they are used for, this is the last type of loan I would like to write about. Commercial real estate loans. In all of my time in the loan business, I have never come across this type of loan or done one, so my knowledge is based on what my colleagues have shared with me and what I have found online. A commercial real estate loan is usually used to buy commercial real estate such as shopping centers, office buildings, industrial buildings, etc. These loans usually require an individual to put a 20%-30% down payment of the purchase price, and the rate is usually tied to the labor index. The loan terms of a commercial real estate loan range between 5-20 years; however, like an adjustable rate mortgage, a lender could extend a longer amortization schedule, for example, 30 years. That would mean that you could have a commercial real estate loan with a fixed rate for 7 years but 30 year term. The process of applying for a commercial real estate loan could be difficult, and it is highly recommended to go through a broker who knows what they are doing in this regard.

One of the most important things in the loan process is Underwriting. Underwriting is the process by which the lender decides whether an individual is worthy and able to repay their loan obligation in the event that they are extended the loan by the lender. Today, many lenders have automated the process, but here are the main aspects a lender is looking for before they extend any amount of loan. It is called the three C's. The three C's stand for Credit, Collateral (capital), Capacity. I will explain each one so you get an understanding of what each "C" means.

- Credit: Credit is when a lender looks at a potential borrower's credit report that has accumulated a history of that individual's payments or non-payments to various creditors.
- Collateral, aka capital: is the assets an individual possesses, such as cash, real property, investments, etc.
- Capacity: This "C" makes sure a borrower has the ability to pay back the loan based on the debts the individual has and the income that he or she produces. It is the calculation of the DTI, known as debt to debt-to-income ratio.

Now that we know what the "C"'s are, we could say that underwriting is basically a measure financial institutions take to make sure they lend to an individual who will have the ability to repay the loan that is going to be extended to them. It is the most important step in the loan process and the borrower must provide all necessary documents in a timely manner; otherwise, they face the risk of their loan getting declined. Underwriting has become very efficient in the last few years, and some lenders have automated the process. However, not every lender has the same underwriting guidelines. Some lenders might be more stringent than others. Usually, the lenders that have more stringent requirements have better loan terms and rates. The lenders who have loose underwriting guidelines usually have higher rates and terms that might not be beneficial to a borrower. Keep in mind that every time you apply for a loan, no matter what type of loan you are applying for, you will always go through an underwriting process.

Processing a loan is the step that comes after the loan is Underwritten. It is the process that the lenders take a look at all the documents to make sure nothing is missing. The loan documents also go through a quality control process where the loan documents are authenticated and checked against government records. For example, when you submit your tax returns to a lender for a mortgage, the lender is going to ask for a document known as a 4506, which lets the lender get access to your tax returns.

In the loan process, a lender could ask for additional documents, such as verification of employment or letters of explanation for different issues that might arise during the loan process.

There is a critical step in the loan process and that is locking in the rate. This term is used when the borrower would submit a document requesting the lender lock in the interest rate for the loan at that days rate. Rate locks are usually set for a thirty-day period and could be locked for forty-five days at an additional cost. Rate locks are crucial because they guarantee that the rate won't change for the period of time that the rate was locked in for; therefore, it is crucial to close the loan within the rate lock period. This is because if you don't and rates increase, you would have to relock the rate at the higher market rate. However, if rates drop, you can take advantage of the lower rate as well. Appraisals are another thing to look out for; you might think that the property you are refinancing or purchasing is worth a certain amount of money but in reality, that value could vary greatly from what you initially expected.

If the value is higher than that works for your benefit. However, if the value for the property is lthanthan it could possibly throw a wrench in your loan process, and you might have to revise your loan amount or even come up with extra funds to make up for the difference. These issues arise more frequently than people expect. More often than not, values are usually lower than what we believe them to be. Many people also believe that if they have done remodeling, then their properties would increase substantially in value; it is true that there will be an increase in their property value, however, that value is often not as high as you would expect. I have seen this happen firsthand, and property owners become furious; therefore I want to set an expectation that if you are remodeling with a hope of a substantial increase in your property value, then that is a false narrative that needs to stop. Loan officers also must set expectations regarding property values and let their borrowers know that they will qualify for that loan amount only if the appraisal comes in at the value needed to qualify for the loan amount they are applying for. This is a really crucial point I would like to make because many times loans fall through and don't get funded because appraisals come in lower than what the property owner said it would come in at. Another important point I would like to make is that you should never rely on any website that estimates values. If you would like to get a precise value for your property, you should pay a licensed appraiser to come and do the appraisal for you and in many instances, depending on the lender and how old that appraisal is, you would be able to use the same appraisal for the loan you are applying for.

So, now that you have gone through finding a lender, submitting all the documents necessary and gone through underwriting and the loan process. What comes next?

Well, now you have to close the loan, and closing the loan could at times be the most stressful part because so many things could go wrong. For beginners, the lender might come at you right before closing and ask you for additional documents. The lock on your mortgage rate might expire, and now you would be subject to a higher rate that you can't qualify for and many other contingencies and situations that might come up. So what to do? First and foremost, make sure you communicate with your lender and make sure your lender communicates with you!

If you are using a mortgage broker, make sure they have a good relationship with their lenders and that they are well versed with lenders' guidelines and conditions (this is where it is advantageous to have a mortgage broker). Make sure you provide all of the documents in a timely manner, and if you are working with a mortgage broker, make sure that they submit those documents in a timely manner. Part of the loan process is the closing process, which goes through another step of quality control. The final process of the loan process is when the loan is clear to close, and the documents are drawn. Once documents are drawn, the borrower has to sign those documents, and depending on the type of loan, the funds would either be disbursed directly to the borrower's account or through an escrow company. In the case of mortgages, you will need a notary present to sign all of the loan documents, and the notary will certify all loan documents as well. The lender at this time will transfer the funds to an escrow company and fund the loan. The escrow company's role is to act as a non-biased third-party entity that collects all the funds and documents and then distributes the funds and fees to the parties involved in the loan process. Congratulations, you have funded your loan!

Now that your loan has been funded, no matter the type of loan you have, an individual has the responsibility of paying off that loan. Usually, a lender sets up a payment date by which an individual has to pay their obligation once a month. Lenders have different ways of accepting payments nowadays. A person could pay by check, credit card, debit card, or electronic transfer from their bank account. However, many banks, credit card companies and lenders give the borrower the option of choosing their payment due date. Mortgages usually have a fifteen-day grace period. A grace period is a time during which an individual has to pay their payment without incurring any penalties or fees, as long as they pay before the grace period expires. When making payments, the payment usually consists of the interest portion and the principal portion. A greater portion of the payment is usually applied to the interest of the loan in the beginning stages of the loan, and as more and more payments are applied, a greater portion of the payment is applied to the principal of the loan. This is called amortization, and it is illustrated by the following amortization table:

Loan Summary	
Loan Amount:	300,000.00
Monthly Payment:	$1,610.46
Total # Of Payments:	360
Start Date:	Jun 2020
Payoff Date:	May 2050
Total Interest Paid:	$279,767.35
Total Payment:	$579,767.35

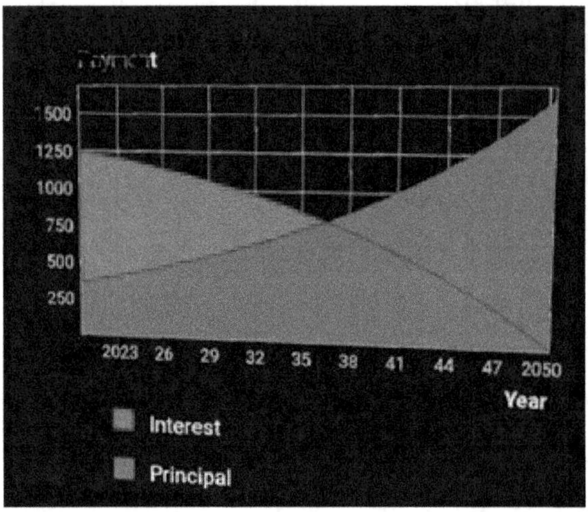

Loan Amortization Schedule

Year	C2	C3	C4	C5	C6	Interest	Principal	Payment	Balance
2020	7	4	1	25	99	$8,718.2	$2,555.0	$11,273	$297,444
2021	12	76	2	58	17	$14,768	$4,556.8	$19,325	$292,888
2022	12	63	5	58	22	$14,535	$4,789.9	$19,325	$288,098
2023	12	56	5	58	22	$14,290	$5,035.0	$19,325	$283,063
2024	12	96	1	58	21	$14,032	$5,292.6	$19,325	$277,770
2025	12	18	1	58	59	$13,762	$5,563.3	$19,325	$272,207
2026	12	55	9	58	20	$13,477	$5,848.0	$19,325	$266,359
2027	12	35	3	58	17	$13,178	$6,147.2	$19,325	$260,211
2028	12	85	2	58	94	$12,863	$6,461.7	$19,325	$253,750
2029	12	26	3	58	21	$12,533	$6,792.3	$19,325	$246,957
2030	12	75	2	58	89	$12,185	$7,139.8	$19,325	$239,818
2031	12	46	3	58	06	$11,820	$7,505.1	$19,325	$232,312
2032	12	48	2	58	94	$11,436	$7,889.0	$19,325	$224,423
2033	12	86	9	58	85	$11,032	$8,292.7	$19,325	$216,131
2034	12	59	2	58	13	$10,608	$8,716.9	$19,325	$207,414
2035	12	61	9	58	15	$10,162	$9,162.9	$19,325	$198,251
2036	12	2	6	58	42	$9,693	$9,631.7	$19,325	$188,619
2037	12	4	54	58	88	$9,201	$10,124	$19,325	$178,494
2038	12	5	53	58	36	$8,683	$10,642	$19,325	$167,852
2039	12	6	02	58	34	$8,138.5	$11,187	$19,325	$156,665
2040	12	1	37	58	97	$7,566.2	$11,759	$19,325	$144,905
2041	12	8	00	58	97	$6,964.5	$12,361	$19,325	$132,544
2042	12	7	41	58	55	$6,332.1	$12,993	$19,325	$119,551
2043	12	0	18	58	37	$5,667.4	$13,658	$19,325	$105,893
2044	12	2	96	58	1	$4,968.6	$14,356	$19,325	$91,536.4
2045	12	9	49	58	2	$4,234.0	$15,091	$19,325	$76,444.9
2046	12	8	60	58	2	$3,461.9	$15,863	$19,325	$60,581.3
2047	12	7	21	58	1	$2,650.3	$16,675	$19,325	$43,906.1
2048	12	3	35	58	7	$1,797.2	$17,528	$19,325	$26,377.7
2049	12	13	58			$900.45	$18,425	$19,325	$7,952.64

The table and payment schedule above also illustrate how banks make money and how lucrative lending is for banks. Therefore, this ties in nicely with how you would also understand the way banks and lending institutions work from previous chapters. Finding a loan calculator is fairly easy, and I recommend Jecale. That is what I used for the above illustration. The illustration above also shows how much interest you are paying over the life of the loan therefore, when the economy is going through a time of low interest rates it is wise to purchase a house even though the real estate market might dictate higher purchase prices the long term savings are higher because you will end up spending much less on interest than you would if interest rates were higher.

Failure to pay a loan carries consequence. In this section, I will spell out what those consequences are and what you could do about them or not. First and foremost, we must understand that a loan must be repaid. It is each person's responsibility to pay back the debt that they take out. Many people hold different opinions on this matter, and it is open to debate whether lending institutions and banks engage in ethical lending practices. Nevertheless, individuals have an obligation to repay their debt. I will start by giving examples of the most common debts that individuals carry and the consequences of not paying that debt, and if there are any remedies. In some instances, the remedies are temporary and require a more permanent solution, which I will address later. However, before I start in most cases your FICO rating will always be affected negatively when you don't pay your debt.

I am going to start with Credit card debt because, in my opinion, this is where most people fail to pay their debts, and their financial difficulties begin. Failing to pay your credit card debt results in your fico score dropping and will most definitely affect it negatively. If an individual falls behind for a month, they will most likely get charged a late fee and be reported to the credit agencies. They are sure to also see an immediate negative impact on their credit scores. This will happen for the first three months if an individual does not pay their credit card fees. Along with late fees, credit card companies will increase the interest rates and tack it on the balance. This is where people fall into the trap of credit card debt and the never-ending cycle of owing money and never getting out of it. In my humble opinion this is an evil practice of entrapping people into financial ruin, especially if that person is just starting out in life. I also understand that part of the responsibility falls on the individual, and an individual should never spend more than what he/she can afford. However, for the credit card companies to exploit people's emotional and financial weakness or lack of knowledge is evil! Now, here is what the creditor will do depending on the balance: the creditor will send your credit card bill to a collection agency, and if the collection agency is unsuccessful in collecting, the creditor might have their law firm contact you and threaten you with lawsuits, and some creditors do take individuals to court. However, there is light at the end of the tunnel. An individual could try and settle the debt, and this is what I mean. An individual could ask the creditor to lower the principal owed and make arrangements to pay for that new balance. An individual may also ask the creditor to waive all of the late fees and interest fees and to also make arrangements for paying back the original balance.

I have done many arrangements like this in the past and have paid 20 to 30 cents on the dollar. There are also credit card counseling services that could talk to creditors on your behalf and come up with similar arrangements, as well as for-profit companies that do the same. However, I found it most efficient to do it yourself. If all else fails, then you will have to go to court and face the judge. One defense argument I have heard that works is that you could tell the judge that you offered a settlement option to the creditor, and the creditor refused to negotiate, and that is why you are in court. Judges will look at that favorably as long as you can prove it. Therefore, always take notes about dates and times that you spoke to creditors or their counsel. Please keep in mind that I do not encourage this practice, and I had to resort to it because of a substantial loss of income or some other financial difficulties; other than that, whenever I have credit card debt, I pay my obligations on time and in full. Bankruptcy is a more permanent and quicker solution because, in some instances and depending on the type of bankruptcy you will file, it will erase your credit card obligation but will devastate your credit rating for seven years. I recommend talking to an attorney regarding the bankruptcy option.

Mortgage debt: Let's face it, mortgages are monstrous loan amounts that take a large chunk of our income to pay back over many years, and if we are faced with a loss of income due to a job loss or health issues, we could face foreclose because we lack the income to pay that monthly payment. So, what happens when we fail to pay a mortgage? Like everything else, your credit score will take an immediate hit. The lending institution will report the non-payment immediately, and the credit bureaus, like good servants, will report it immediately on your credit report, which will result in a decrease in your credit scores. After three months of non-payments, you will receive letters and calls from the lender asking for payment. In some cases, even late fees and threats of foreclosure. The lender will then start with the foreclosure proceedings. Here is where a person could delay the foreclosure or try to get a more permanent solution. Refinancing is always a solution, especially if you can get a favorable rate, which will reduce your mortgage payment. This is the most favorable solution. However, if the foreclosure proceedings start, you could try to negotiate a loan modification. I am not going to go through the process of loan modifications, but in short, a loan modification is when you provide the lender a bunch of paperwork like tax returns, bank statements, etc.; basically, the same documents you used when first applying for your mortgage.

The lender would then proceed to review your paperwork in order to come up with terms that are usually more favorable to the borrower. For example, a lower rate translates to a lower monthly payment, a longer loan term (instead of 30 years, it would be extended to 40 years), or a combination of both. In some rare cases, the lender would also reduce the principal balance; however, that usually happens when the house is worth less than what is owed on the property. In some cases, a loan modification would be rejected. When this happens, the other option might be to file for bankruptcy, and you should discuss this option with your attorney. When filing for bankruptcy, it would stop all foreclosure proceedings for a period of time. In some cases, the bankruptcy could force the bank into a loan modification, but that is not always the case. Therefore, bankruptcy would only delay the foreclosure proceeding and assist you in buying some time and hopefully resolve the issue with the lender. A short sale is another solution; a short sale is when you would sell your property for less than what you owe. This would require the consent of your lender, and you would need to have the property appraised by the lender and prove that the property is worth less than what you owe. If all else fails, the bank will foreclose on your property and will make you leave the premises. They will then assume ownership of the property. This is another permanent solution if you default on your mortgage payment. If you opt to give up on the property and let the lender foreclose on the property, then be prepared to have a devastating reduction in your credit scores and a foreclosure on your credit file for seven years. If you file for bankruptcy to try and save your property, expect the same outcome.

Personal loans: personal loans are almost identical to credit card debt and have the same consequences and solutions. The only difference is that you would receive a lump sum of the money up front when you first take out the loan. So, for example, if you get approved for a ten-thousand-dollar personal loan, you will receive that amount. With credit cards, you can use the credit amount that you got over time. For example, if you have a ten-thousand-dollar credit line, you don't need to use all of that amount. You could use a part of it. Now you could also apply for a personal line of credit, which works like a credit card. The consequences of not paying a personal loan or personal line of credit is the same as a credit card: a hit to your credit score, collection agencies calling, and possible lawsuits if you can't resolve the issue with the lender. Like credit cards, you should negotiate a settlement or a way to make it easier to pay off the loan or line of credit. You always have the option of bankruptcy as well, but that should be a last resort.

Vehicle loan: Most people get their car note through the dealer they purchased their car from. However, you could get a more favorable car loan through a bank or credit union. You just apply for the loan before you start shopping for the vehicle, and take your pre-approval to the dealer. Vehicle loans could be for a variety of vehicles: cars, motorcycles, RVs, boats, recreational vehicles, etc.

Not paying for your vehicle loan could result in the repossession of your vehicle and a hit to your credit score. The best way to resolve the issue with your vehicle loan is to call the lender and ask them to give you some time to pay the payment, and possibly make new payment arrangements. You could also try looking for another lender that could possibly offer a lower rate on your vehicle loan, essentially refinancing your vehicle loan, or you could just sell your car and pay off your loan.

Student loans have been a subject of political debate and a controversial subject in society. People often take out student loans to finance their studies at higher education institutes or some technical schools.

Student loans don't have to be repaid as long as you are in school, but as soon as you finish your schooling, the lenders start calling to make arrangements to pay for your student loans. In some cases, you could ask for forbearance; however, you would need a really good reason to get a forbearance. If you don't pay your student loan, expect to get harassed constantly; you could try and refinance your student loan and get a lower rate, or you could also try to ask the lender to work with you on a lower payment. Bankruptcy is not an option for student loans, although I have heard that some people have wiped clean many student loans through bankruptcy. I don't know how, but an experienced bankruptcy lawyer might know how. The consequences for not paying your student loan are that you will suffer constant harassment from the lenders and collection agencies. A huge hit to your credit scores and the possibility of court proceedings and lawsuits. The student loan system could be a blessing or a curse, depending on what you decide to stud. I your subject of study is in demand when you graduate, it will help you find a job and start your career. If you are not fortunate enough to find a job when you graduate from a job, student loans could be a start to financial ruin because it would most definitely affect your credit profile and your ability to get future loans, and it could set you up for a very hard start in life. I highly recommend that young people take out student loans only if they are certain that they will finish their schooling and that they will choose a profession that is in demand. I am going to voice my opinion: liberal arts, communication, and similar degrees are useless in today's society. Going to school and taking a student loan is a big responsibility, and taking a loan for a useless degree could spell disastrous, especially if you are just starting out. I highly recommend taking student loans for medical school, engineering, dental school, law school or architecture. These professions will always be in demand. Just make sure you follow through and graduate. That is my recommendation and solution to survive a student loan debacle, especially when you are just starting out in life. Good Luck!

Hard money lenders are usually private lenders that have no patience or tolerance for non-payment, that's why hard money loans are short-term loans. The consequence of not paying a hard money loan is basic: foreclosure! The hard money lenders don't negotiate or give you a chance, they move quick and swiftly and start the foreclosure proceedings right away. Trying to negotiate with a hard money lender is usually useless and a waste of time. The best way to resolve the issue with a hard money lender is to refinance the loan with a more conventional loan or sell the property and pay back the loan. Those are pretty much the only options you have. Hard money loans are usually used to flip a house, which is a whole subject by itself, which I am not going to get into, but there is plenty of information online on how to flip annoyed and make some money.

Business loans are guaranteed by collateral and by personal guaranteed, and in some cases, other assets you might own. Failing to pay your business loan would mean a seizure of what you guaranteed. SBA loans could even foreclose on your house if you own one. What is recommended if you can't make the original payment,? Then you should call the lender and try to make arrangements; otherwise, they will seize equipment and assets your business owns.

TYPES OF BANKS

Well, there are so many different banks out there. In this chapter, I will explain the different roles each type of bank plays in our lives. Mygoal is for individuals to understand the role each type of bank has in our daily lives. I will also dive into the benefits and negative aspects of each bank.

The first type of bank I would like to start with is retail banks. A retail bank is the bank that we see on every street corner. Some famous retail banks are Chase Bank, Bank of America, Citibank, and Wells Fargo Bank. In the retail banks, you could open checking and savings accounts, apply for personal loans, mortgages, and auto loans. Most retail banks also have a private banking department for individuals with a high net worth. Retail banks also have investment bankers. Now that you know what a retail bank offers, it will give a more robust understanding of the role they play in our society. As I mentioned, big box banks are everywhere, and this is a major benefit of banking with big retail banks, due to their accessibility. However, this also makes them impersonal and full of regulations and policies. These big box banks also have a high overhead, which translates into higher interest rates on loans and lower interest rates on deposit and investment accounts. Another major issue big retail banks have is high employee turn over and that is why it is very difficult to find good bankers in the big box retail banks. All retail banks are FDIC-insured.

The next type of bank I would like to talk about is the community banks. These banks often have very few branches; in some instances, even one sole branch. They usually serve a certain community and target a need in that community. Community banks are great because you get personalized service and it has a family feeling. The staff at the community bank often knows you on a first-name basis. However, the fees to maintain and conduct transactions at a community bank could be higher than a retail bank. Another issue community banks have is that access to them is very limited, making it very hard to get access to your funds. In short, community banks are great if you are looking for a more personalized experience, but a lack of accessibility might be an issue. Some community banks would offer you access to other banks' ATM machines so you could make certain transactions, and they would waive any fees associated with those transactions.

Credit Unions are like retail banks, but the only difference is that the owners of the credit unions are the depositors and the borrowers of the institutions; also, credit unions are not insured by the FDIC, they are insured by the NCUA (National Credit Union Administration), which is like the FDIC and was created by Congress in the 1970s. Credit Unions are nonprofit institutions. They usually try to keep overhead low, so they have fewer branches and like community banks, they might even have just one branch. Some Credit Unions have membership criteria as well; Credit Unions might require you to belong to a certain group or employer in order to transact with their institution. Credit Unions have fewer product offerings but, but in many cases, have more attractive rates for their credit products. Credit Unions are best known for their low rates on auto loans and home equity lines of credit. Like community banks, credit unions have accessibility issues, but in many cases, they will waive ATM fees at other banks. I personally worked at the Los Angeles Police Federal Credit Union many years ago while I was in college, and I remember the criteria was that you had to be working for the LAPD or be a family member of someone who worked for the LAPD. I also remember that members of this LAPFCU enjoyed free checking accounts and great rates on credit products such as mortgages and auto loans.

Credit Unions function like banks do, but have fewer product offerings; however, like community banks, they are more personable in their service.

Online banks have a special place in my heart because this is where my banking and mortgage career really started. I worked for ING Direct, a pioneer in online banking, and they were known for their savings account because they gave a much higher interest rate than traditional banks. Nowadays, there are several online banks that offer more or less the same rates. Even retail banks are now offering online banking and app-based functions to make people's lives easier to manage their finances. Online banks are able to offer higher rates on deposit accounts because they have less overhead and expenses as a result, they are also able to offer lower rates on credit products. There are certain online banks that are completely virtual and don't have any physical presence; the only way to get access to your funds is through ATM's. While working at ING Direct, they would link your savings account to your current checking account (Wells Fargo, Bank of America, Chase), so you would link your ING Direct savings account and transfer money to and from your accounts. Loan payments would also be made either from your linked checking account or savings account.

Most banks as mentioned before, now a day's offer many services online, like bill pay, transferring money between accounts, even transferring money between one individual to another using their phone number (Zelle), some banks even offer wire transfer capabilities online, and with technological improvements, you can now deposit checks through your banking app. Online banking is great because it has encouraged people to avoid the in-person banking and transferred many of the banking functions to the virtual realm. I foresee that in the future, almost all banking will be done virtually, and there will be no need for physical bank locations. However, it will take away from the personal relationship banking and knowledge shared by individuals about money management and banking in general.

Investment banks are institutions that help individuals with financial advice in transactions relating to securities and stocks. The individuals who work at investment banks usually assist their clients with how and where they should invest their money so that they can get the highest return on their investment. Investment banks also help individuals who usually have a high net worth. Bankers who assist these individuals are licensed with several licenses, which are governed by the state and federal regulators (life insurance license, Series 6,7,63,65). Examples of investment banks would be Merrill Lynch, Charles Schwab, and private banking divisions at some retail banks. Keep in mind that investing in the stock market carries risk, and nothing is guaranteed and there is no FDIC insurance on investment accounts.

TYPES OF ACCOUNTS

In this chapter we will delve into different types of bank accounts and their uses and functions. I will also explain their strengths and weaknesses when appropriate. You should always do your own research at your local banks to see what type of account would be most appropriate for your situation. Talking to your banker and telling him your situation and asking questions about bank account fees and restrictions is always a good idea, so you won't be caught by surprise and start complaining. Having the knowledge which nowadays is readily available is important so that you won't fall into a bank account that is not suitable to your situation. I can't emphasize enough the importance of asking your banker questions and making sure you choose the right account. Another important aspect when you choose a bank account is that you should always shop around different banks to make sure that the bank has the features and services that suit you best. You should also be ready to provide personal identifying documentation when opening a bank account. With any bank account, you will need certain types of documents to open an account; each bank differs with their requirements, and a banker will tell you what you will need to open the account you want to open. Some banks also offer accounts to foreign nationals.

Now, let's get started with the types of accounts banks usually offer and keep in mind this is a broad overview.

Checking accounts/debit cards: This is the most common account that almost every person has. It is the most accessible account, and it is usually used to pay bills, cover shopping, manage expenses, and budget individual and family finances. Checking accounts are popular because almost every bank offers them, but not all checking accounts are created equal. Some banks will offer free checking accounts, while others will have fees unless you meet certain stipulations. Some of the stipulations you might have to meet to waive a checking account fee might include a minimum monthly balance (could be an average monthly balance or at all times), transferring a certain amount of money automatically from your checking account to your saving account, making a certain amount of transactions with your debit card, online bill pay, etc. each bank is different therefore you should talk to your banker at your local bank so you know what it would take to waive those fees. Checking accounts come with debit cards or ATM cards.

Debit cards have a Visa or MasterCard logo on it and could be used at any business or merchant that accepts Visa or MasterCard.

This is really convenient because the money comes out of your checking account directly and it is recorded to your statement and account summary, which you could access online or through your bank's app if they offer one. Debit cards have daily limits at ATM's, they usually tap out at three hundred dollars a day for normal checking accounts and could go higher if you request it or are a private client at the bank, or a preferred client at the bank. Another benefit of checking accounts is that most banks offer online bill pay, where you can enter your creditors' information on your bank's online portal or app and set up automatic bill payments to those creditors. Checking accounts are liquid, meaning that you have access to your funds or money at any time. However, if you make a deposit into your checking account with a check or checks, those funds might go on hold for a certain period of time. The hold depends on several factors such as the length of time the account has been open, the current balance, the average monthly balance, and deposit amounts, and whether the check is local or from a different state. Each bank has its own criteria, and that criteria could differ from one bank to another. One way to try to avoid a hold on a check is to have a banker or teller call the bank. The check is drawn on to verify the availability of funds for the check in question. Banks also prefer cashier checks, bank checks, and money orders; the hold time on those is usually less than traditional checks. An individual is also able to purchase checks from their bank if they have a checking account to pay for different expenses. The advantage of paper checks is that you have a paper trail, and it promotes record keeping. The disadvantage is that paper checks are becoming obsolete with advances in technology, as well as online bill pay and functions like Zelle and PayPal. In chapter four, I spoke about how you should utilize your checking account and manage your money and budgets. Some banks offer interest bearing checking accounts. These interest-bearing checking accounts could carry higher fees and might have certain stipulations, so be aware of that. Some banks will start giving you interest on your checking account if you reach a certain balance, and that balance varies from one bank to another.

Another aspect to keep in mind when it comes to checking accounts is that this type of account is always evolving, and as technological advances take place and government regulations come into place, the checking account changes as well. For example, the checking account is shifting from paper checks to online bill pay and app-based payment options. The ATM machine has also changed in the past. The ATM had very few functions but was mainly used to withdraw money using an ATM card that was linked to your checking account. With technological advancements and government interference in wage policy, ATMs added more features so people have less interactions with bank personnel. As a result, many banks cut their personnel, and many of the transactions could now be done by using the ATM.

For example: transferring funds from one account to another, Deposit cash and checks, checking balances, withdrawing cash, etc.

ATM cards at most banking institutions have been replaced by Debit cards that carry the Visa and MasterCard logos, and as I mentioned previously, could be used at any merchant or business that accepts these cards. Another benefit of a checking account nowadays is that if you experience any fraudulent activity, you could report it to the bank and the bank would start an investigation. Debit cards, in some instances, have a purchase limit even if you have enough money to cover the purchase or expense; in this case, you will have to contact your bank and request a higher limit and notify them of the transaction. I will give an example of what happened to me; I made a purchase that was out of the ordinary with my debit card and received a text message with an email asking me to click on the link to verify the purchase before it went the transaction went through. So, as we see, the banks are taking measures to protect consumers against fraudulent activity.

Another aspect to keep in mind about your checking account is when you travel; depending on where you are traveling to you could use your debit card or ATM card to withdraw money at foreign banks. There might be fees that you might have to pay, but in general, the exchange rates when withdrawing from an ATM are more favorable. Another important thing to consider when traveling is to inform your bank that you are traveling and let them know where you are going, so that if you make a purchase with your debit card or use an ATM, your bank is aware of this. It has happened to me personally. When I traveled and failed to alert my bank of my traveling plans, my debit card purchases got declined, and I had to make a call to my bank to remedy the situation. The bank might ask you additional security questions to verify that they are talking to the account holder, but this is to safeguard against fraud and theft. Banks do this to safeguard their clients because, in recent years, there has been massive fraud, so banks protect their customers this way.

To conclude, checking accounts are the most common, and if you do banking, you probably have one. Checking accounts are convenient in that they offer features that help us in our daily life and are crucial in managing our money and paying our expenses and creditors. As technology evolves, so does banking and the checking account has evolved from its early days of paper checks to being app-based and online.

Savings accounts: Savings accounts are meant to be a monetary vehicle for individuals to save money. The money saved could be saved for different purposes, and it really depends on what that individual has in mind to save for. Therefore, because a savings account is designated as a vehicle to save money, the number of withdrawals an individual could make is limited to six withdrawals per month (Regulation D) with unlimited amounts of deposits. Savings accounts carry an interest rate that is measured by the annual percentage yield (APY). Depending on the bank, the savings account might carry a monthly fee that could possibly be avoided if you meet certain criteria. Most online savings accounts do not have any fees associated with them or any minimum balance requirements. A minor savings account could be opened for any age child, and it could be a great way to save for that child's car and college expenses when they grow up. The minor savings account could be converted to a normal savings account once the individual reaches 16 years of age. In chapter four, I explained how you could utilize your savings account to reach your goals.

Money Market accounts: A money market account is like a savings account; the only difference is that some banks give you a slightly higher rate and let you write checks on that account, usually three checks a month. Money market accounts also require a higher balance than a savings account. I don't think that many banks offer this type of account, and I haven't seen it lately.

Teen checking account: A Teen checking account is exactly like a regular checking account that could be opened by a minor child who is sixteen or older. This account, in most cases, must be opened with an adult, usually a parent or legal guardian. This account comes with a debit card. It is usually free, and when the individual turns eighteen, then the account usually converts to a regular checking account with all the stipulations of the bank's fees and policies for that account. My opinion about teen checking accounts is mixed. On the one hand, it could help a young person start their journey toward financial responsibility and teach them early on how to handle money and develop financial literacy. On the other hand, it could cause a lot of damage for a young person if that individual does not handle his finances responsibly, and he could set himself back monetary wise. Therefore, I recommend parental supervision and setting limits on debit cards and withdrawal amounts. I also recommend that text messages and emails be sent to parents after every purchase, and even better, the parent has to approve the purchase or expense. However, every family is different, and some teens are responsible and want to learn how to manage their finances with a checking account and are disciplined. To conclude, a teen checking account should be considered on a case-by-case basis; based on the family's dynamic and situation.

CDs or Certificate of Deposit: A certificate of deposit is a deposit account where an individual would deposit a set amount of money for a set amount of time and would get a fixed interest rate for the time the money stays in the CD. Now, the longer the duration of the CD, the higher the interest rate. If an individual decides to withdraw the CD prematurely, the individual could face fees and penalties for "breaking the CD". You cannot add funds to A CD; if you wanted to add funds, you would have to open a new CD at current market rates.

CDs offer higher rates because an individual doesn't have access to those funds. CDs usually come in 3, 6, 9, 12, 18, 24, 36, 48, 60-month periods. CDs are usually FDIC insured. While working at the bank, I used a customer's CD as collateral for a line of credit. I even had a customer open a CD and then qualified him for a line of credit, using the CD as collateral. CDs are a straightforward account and are great for risk-averse individuals that want their money in a safe instrument where they can earn some interest and have no need for those funds in the foreseeable future. Something I learned while working at the online bank is that, let's say you have $10,000 that you want to place in a very safe investment but would like to have some liquidity; then you would open five different CDs ranging from one year to five years and in each CD you would deposit $2,000. Each year, one of the CDs would mature and you would earn interest and have access to your funds.

The CD is a great instrument to diversify one's investments.

Trust Account: I am not going to get into the mechanics of what a trust is and what it is used for because it has nothing to do with banking. What I will go into is what a trust account role is in banking and what you will need to open a trust account; so let's get started. A trust account is usually opened by an individual to stop probate and taxation after death. It is usually managed by a lawyer who is hired to execute the trust on behalf of the individual and the beneficiary of the trust account. When opening the trust account, the bank will require all documentation in regard to the trust, and there are no ifs or buts about it. There are two types of trust accounts: revocable and an irrevocable trust account. The difference has to do with tax consequences, which are different for each individual and should be discussed with your tax person or accountant. I personally don't think that trust accounts are necessary because you should just add the person you want to list as an heir on the account as a joint account owner. This will also help avoid probate and you could also help pay for any medical expenses while that person is alive. Trust accounts are ok if a person has no heirs and he is planning to leave his money for a nonprofit organization or some other purpose, but if you are planning on leaving your funds to a family member or person just add them to your account (save yourself the headache).

Retirement Accounts: A retirement account is a

savings account with the goal of saving money for when one reaches their retirement age. There are other retirement vehicles that banks offer, like IRA (individual retirement account) accounts that have limits on the annual contributions. Roth IRA accounts which basically means money that was already taxed, are being contributed to the account, or you have pre-taxed income that is contributed to your account. The benefit of pretax money is that you can save more now, but you will be taxed later when you withdraw the money upon retirement. The theory behind this is that by the time you retire, your tax bracket would be lowered, therefore you would pay less taxes than if you paid into the IRA after deducting taxes. This is something that many people don't know, but you could also open 401k accounts for individuals. 401 (k)'s have higher contribution limits and other features IRA accounts don't have. I will not get into 401(k) s because banks usually don't offer them; you could discuss 401 (k) s with your financial advisor or private banker. Other retirement vehicles could be life insurance policies, annuities, and mutual funds. These accounts carry risks if they are tied to the stock market or securities; therefore, I highly recommend you talk to somebody who has the appropriate licenses. Life insurance policies are not always connected to the stock market and have generous returns, so talking to a life insurance agent is a great idea because a life insurance policy is two-pronged, it has a retirement option and a life policy that would pay out a sum of money to your loved ones upon death. Each of these products has its own intricacies; therefore, please talk to an expert in the industry in where field you are looking to invest in for your retirement.

Investment accounts (Brokerage accounts): Investment accounts are accounts that contain stocks, bonds, and securities. These accounts carry a risk of losing money and are not insured by the FDIC. These accounts are usually for people who trade in stocks, futures, and bonds. These accounts at banks are usually handled by a private banker or a licensed banker. Some examples of investment accounts would be an account at Charles Schwab, Merrill Lynch, E*TRADE, etc. Make sure that the person you are talking to is knowledgeable enough in the securities market because it is a risky market at times.

Business accounts, Merchant accounts, Payroll accounts: I decided to group these accounts because they are related to one another and they work in Unison. Business accounts, like its name ,serve business owners in their banking, and many banks have business bankers to serve the business community. Business accounts do have fees, and also in certain cases, additional requirements. I highly recommend you talk with a business banker about a business account and what you could do to avoid fees on business accounts. Business accounts also come with checks, and many of the business account functions are the same as a consumer checking account; the only difference is that a business account can accept merchant account deposits and payroll withdrawals. Banks also offer online banking and online bill pay, so you can manage your business account online. Credit unions and community banks also offer business accounts, and they might have better terms than retail banks. A business owner could also open a business savings account, which acts the same way a traditional savings account works, but it works in conjunction with a business checking account. To open a business account, you will need documents showing that you opened a business with the county you live in or the state you are doing business in. Therefore, if it is a DBA, usually for a sole proprietorship (Doing business as), you will need the county documents showing that you are set to do business. Some banks will also ask for a tax ID document. If it is a corporation (Inc.) or limited liability company (LLC),, you will need the state documents to open a business account. Again, you might need tax documentation as well, and each bank is different in regard to. The way a merchant account plays a role with the business account is that if you are a business owner, you will need to have a merchant account to process credit card transactions in your business, only if your business requires it. Merchant accounts are accounts that settle payments from credit and debit transactions. When these transactions take place, depending on who your merchant processor is, the money would be deposited into your business account after fees and percentages are deducted from each merchant processing transaction.

A business owner should always shop for the best rates for merchant processing because banks don't always offer the best rates; in fact, they are usually much higher than smaller merchant processing businesses. Even though a merchant account with a bank will most likely waive your business account fees, it still does not justify the savings you would get by going with another merchant service processor, and besides, there are other ways to avoid business account fees. A Payroll account is when you hire a company to handle your payroll. Usually, the payroll account is a separate account that a business would use to pay wages to its employees through a business account. There are many payroll companies, and as a business owner, you should see which payroll company would work best for you, since each payroll company offers different features at different prices. Some payroll companies offer a bundle of services where you could get your payroll and HR services through them as well. To open a business checking or saving account, you will need to show your ID and documentation from the city, county, or state you are doing business in. You could use the same concept in chapter four with your business accounts, and these concepts would be perfect if you work in a business where you have to keep separate accounts for different functions without comingling funds. Many banks offer online functions for business owners to use, like normal consumer accounts. Merchant processors and payroll companies offer online functions as well as apps to track your merchant deposits and payroll transactions. To conclude, business accounts, merchant accounts, and payroll accounts are crucial in running a business because they serve as instruments to control the business's cash flow and control its expenses.

ChexSystems: Like the three credit reporting companies I wrote about previously, Chex Systems is a consumer reporting agency that collects information about closed checking and savings accounts. The banks also report to ChexSystems if the account was closed due to fraud or account was closed due to being overdrawn. When opening a bank account, many financial institutions check the ChexSystems database to ensure you are in good standing before you can open a bank account. However, there are some banks that would allow you to open a bank account with restrictions. Some of the restrictions you might face: Automatic hold on any check deposit, limits on the number of monthly checks you can write, limits on Debit card transactions, and limits on withdrawal amounts. These restricted accounts could eventually convert to a traditional account, and each bank has its own parameters. Chex Systems was put in place to make sure people are held responsible for managing their accounts and to avoid fraud in banking. However, many bank practices cause good individuals to overdraw their accounts. Even though some banks were fined large sums of money and some banking reforms in regards to overdraft fees and policies, many people still fall victim to banks' questionable practices when it comes to overdraft policies and procedures. I wrote about ways to avoid overdraft fees in chapter four, and I highly recommend you read about them. Now, if you involve yourself in deliberate fraud then you deserve to be on ChexSystems and further prosecution from the authorities as well.

OTHER FINANCIAL INVESTMENTS AND VEHICLES

In this chapter I am going to delve into some topics that are not necessarily connected to banking but are absolutely essential to your personal finance and your financial well-being.

I touched on life insurance briefly before, and I would like to get into it in more detail. Life insurance is very important, especially if you have a family and own an asset or asset that has a debt attached to it, like a mortgage or any sort of loan. The purpose of a life insurance policy is to protect your loved ones financially in case of death. A life insurance policy would carry a death benefit that would pay a lump sum to your beneficiary or beneficiaries upon your passing. A beneficiary could be your spouse, children, parent, or someone who is close to you, or you care about. If the life insurance proceeds are to be paid to your estate, your creditors might lay claim to the proceeds, but if the proceeds are to be paid directly to your beneficiaries, ingeneral, the creditors won't have a claim to those funds. Life insurance policies have different types of features and benefits that you should discuss with a life insurance agent, aka a financial planner. The reason I am saying that you should check with a licensed life insurance agent is that each insurance company has different products, and your life insurance agent would/should help you choose the best features that are best for you. There are several types of life insurance policies, and I will explain the ones that are the most popular.

Term Life Policy: Also known as a term policy. This policy carries a death benefit that is set for a certain number of years (10, 20, 30 years), and the policy owner would pay the premium for this policy, and when the policy term ends, the policy terminates unless the insurance company allows you to extend it. This policy could carry additional benefits, which you should discuss with your life insurance agent.

Whole Life Policy: This is what most people use to save for their retirement outside their 401k's and IRAs. This kind of policy carries on until death or until you stop paying for it. Like a term policy, it has a death benefit, but it also carries a savings aspect where after-tax money is saved into the life insurance policy and upon retirement, you would get access to the funds.

The beauty of a whole life policy is that it has a guaranteed rate of return and some additional benefits that could be attached to it. Financial planners often times would make illustrations showing you how much money you would save if you started saving now until retirement. There are several analyses that they use to determine the death benefit and which varies from one person to another.

Variable life policy: It is exactly the same as a whole life policy, the only difference is that the life insurance agent must carry additional licenses, and the investment part of it carries risk of losing money because it is tied to the stock market.

Final Expense policies: A final expense policy is a policy that has a smaller death benefit that is bought to cover burial costs only. It could carry other benefits, and it should be discussed with your financial planner.

Life insurance is great, and in my opinion, everyone should have a life insurance policy no matter what, especially if you have a family and even more so if you have any debt whatsoever!! I am a licensed life and health agent in 10 states and when I do financial advising, I dig deep. I do a complete audit of your financial life and I recommend products that will fit your lifestyle and your specific needs. I ask questions and listen to you I uncover your pain and then I make recommendations based on what you need. I always look out for my clients' best interests and take a consultative approach. Therefore, make sure when you choose your financial advisor that you choose someone who is looking out for your best interest or best financial wellbeing.

The Stock market is where fortunes could be made, or you could lose your shirt. The stock market is where companies' values are determined by their stock value. Each company on the stock exchange has a certain number of stocks, and each stock has a certain value that is determined by demand, new invention, type of product or service, positive or negative news, and other factors for that stock. Banks, life insurance companies, institutionalized investors, and individuals all trade in the stock market. Many mutual funds, 401k funds, hedge funds, IRAs, etc. Invest in the stock market as well. Investing in the stock market carries risk, but the reward for the risk could be very lucrative if you know how to trade in stocks. There are many resources online for you to money. Explore and learn how to trade the stock market. However, keep in mind the risks involved in trading stocks, as inexperienced traders can lose a significant amount of money if they are not familiar with the market. I personally lost a lot of money in the stock market, and I always advise that unless you know what you are doing, don't invest in the stock market. This is my opinion;, however, if you are investing through a 401k, mutual fund or an IRA, or some other vehicle, you should be fine. Assuming the people who manage these funds are diversifying your funds and are experienced in trading stocks but always keep in mind that you could still lose money! In short, the stock market is another vehicle you should consider, and your banker or financial planner could give you guidance or refer you to the right people. There are many different strategies in trading the stock market, and if you want to learn to trade the stock market, you might be good at it and even make a fortune, but that is up to you.

Foreign exchange, also known as FOREX, Like the stock market, is an exchange where countries' currencies are traded, and trading in the forex exchange could be rewarding or you could lose your shirt as well. Therefore, it is advisable that you know what you are doing and who you trust with your money when trading in the forex market. Usually, people would trade one country's currency against another country's currency; for example, the U.S. Dollar against the Euro (USD vs EUR) or the Japanese Yen against the British Pound. There are so many resources online about trading forex, and forex is also notoriously known for all the scams involved ; therefore, it is very important that you choose a legit broker and trading platform. Forex trading is used by many institutionalized traders, private individuals, and hedge funds etc. Forex trading could be extremely lucrative as well and if you learn it and know how to trade in currencies, you could potentially get rich.

Cryptocurrency, also known as Bitcoin, was launched in the past decade or so, and it is a digital currency that an individual could use to purchase goods and services and also trade. Cryptocurrency uses an online ledger with extremely strong cryptography to secure online transactions. In recent years, the value of Bitcoin has risen tremendously, mostly because of speculation. No one really knows where cryptocurrency is headed, but many people feel that the future of currency is embedded in cryptocurrency. There is ample content about the cryptocurrency market, and I highly recommend that you study it. As of now, banks have not made their position clear on the matter of cryptocurrency, but I am assuming that some of the banks have engaged in cryptocurrency trading or investing.

Life insurance illustration:

Consultation for mortgages, life insurance, financial planning, and financial audits.

CONCLUSION

Since the inception of banks, the economies of the world have changed. What started as a way to store money for people in return for a fee has blown up into an enterprise. I hope that by writing this book I have provided you with a means to understand banking, how banks work and how you could use the banking system to better your finances and economic wellbeing.

To conclude, I have mixed feelings about banking and the banking institutions. On one hand, they serve as a way for us to leverage our money and use the credit they extend to us for our benefit; and on the other hand, I feel that banks have an unfair advantage and too much power in controlling our economy and subsequently our lives. The fact that banks are engaged in frictional lending is outrageous by itself! The fact that banks give us low interest rates and gauge us on credit card rates is outrageous as well. However, without banks we wouldn't be able to borrow money to buy real estate and invest in different types of opportunities. For those of you who are pro-government control (Socialists, Communists), the government wouldn't be able to keep tabs on your income for taxation purposes without a banking system. I am also noticing that there is a consolidation of banking, meaning that there are fewer banks, which decreases competition and limits our choices of where we can do our banking. The issue with this is that less banking competition will mean that the banks will control the types of accounts they offer and give us subpar accounts and services, which will limit our ability to reach our investment goals. Banks have become an integral part of our lives; we use banks for anything from depositing money in our accounts to using bank accounts to conduct business.

Banks have become so vital that they are the only major institution that lends money to individuals for real estate transactions and commerce. There is so much more I could write about banking and all that it encompasses, but that is not the purpose of this book. The purpose of this book is to make sure you have a basic understanding of banks and their functions, and how to use banks to your advantage. I really hope that "Drawers For Your Money: a guide to banking, finance, and financial wellbeing" gave you information and knowledge to use in your daily life, on how to use banks to manage your finances in the future.

ABOUT THE AUTHOR

Nir is an enthusiastic financial planner with over 15 years of experience in the banking industry. He is a dedicated father and advocate for financial literacy.

www.ingramcontent.com/pod-product-compliance
Lightning Source LLC
LaVergne TN
LVHW022225200926
848481LV00006B/2127
9798902220503